VEGETABLES

VEGETABLES

More Than 80 Delicious Recipes for Wonderful Salads, Soups and More

A Fireside Book
Published by Simon & Schuster
New York London Toronto Sydney

Fireside
A Division of Simon & Schuster, Inc.
1230 Avenue of the Americas
New York, NY 10020

First Fireside hardcover edition December 2008

Fireside and colophon are registered trademarks of Simon & Schuster, Inc.

For information about special discounts for bulk purchases,
please contact Simon & Schuster Special Sales
at 1-800-456-6798 or business@simonandschuster.com

Manufactured in China

10   9   8   7   6   5   4   3   2   1

ISBN-13: 978-1-4165-9349-2
ISBN-10:   1-4165-9349-7

Contents

Vegetables

66 Baked Vegetables

122 Vegetables in Salad

Contents

150 Vegetable Soups

Introduction

VEGETABLE SEASONS

Tomatoes, string beans, peppers and eggplants are available on market stalls and in supermarkets all year round. This is mainly owing to greenhouses, which are now commonly used to grow fruit and vegetables, putting an end to the traditional distinction between what is in season and what isn't.

However, this system has its price: vegetables that have not ripened naturally have less flavor, tending towards a watery pulp and, moreover, they contain a high concentration of artificial plant nutrients and fertilizers taken from the soil in which they have grown.

Eating vegetables in season is not, therefore, merely a choice based on quality. Respect for nature might even help safeguard our health.

The following pages contain a calendar that illustrates the seasonality of the most common vegetables.

SPRING

Asparagus

Fresh asparagus must have firm stalks and tightly closed tips. The woody part of the stalk must be gently scraped with a knife prior to cooking. Asparagus should be cooked upright in a tall and narrow pot, with the tips out of the water, for 15-20 minutes.

Carrots

Carrots are used as aromatic vegetables in boiled dishes and in vegetable stock, or can be included in salads, soufflés, timbales and soups. Carrots should be lightly brushed or scraped with a knife; it is better to cut them only just before use to prevent them from browning.

Chicory

This group includes various types of vegetables, including radicchio and Catalogna chicory. The spring varieties are eaten in salads; the winter varieties are excellent when boiled in water for 10-15 minutes and dressed with oil and lemon juice. Chicory should be cleaned by discarding the outer leaves and the bottom part covered in earth and rinsing under running water for a few minutes.

Onions and green onions

Onions and green onions are typical spring vegetables. They can be eaten raw in mixed salads, or sautéed and used as a base for soups or sauces. The top and the outer skin must be removed before eating.

Peas

These legumes are extremely rich in vitamins, proteins and dietary minerals. They make excellent side dishes or can be used to fill timbales and savory pies. To clean, open the pods by hand, pour the seeds into a bowl and rinse under running water.

Lettuce

There are 3 main types of lettuce: Romaine lettuce with long leaves and a firm rib down their centers, loose-leaf lettuce with tender leaves, and head lettuce with rounded leaves that form a tight ball. Lettuce is eaten in salads after being rinsed under running water. Fresh lettuce must have green, crunchy leaves and should be free from any blemish.

Radishes

Radishes are small red or white roots with a slightly pungent flavor. They are eaten in salads and crudités after being rinsed under running water.

Arugula

Arugula is a salad green with a peppery and somewhat bitter flavor; it can be used as an alternative to basil in making pesto. To prepare arugula, remove the stalks after washing and hand-shred the leaves.

SUMMER

Cucumbers

Cucumbers are eaten mainly in summer, and their high water content makes them extremely refreshing. Cucumbers should be carefully peeled (the skin contains a number of beneficial nutrients but is tough and hard to digest) and sliced into thin rounds. To draw out excess moisture, place in a colander and sprinkle with table salt.

String Beans

String beans should be bright green with a firm and crunchy texture. To check their freshness, snap off one of the bean's tips and pull it: if the bean is firm and the tip snaps off neatly, the beans are fresh. In addition, young pods usually do not have any string. String beans should be steam-cooked or boiled in water, and are excellent when added to soups and minestrone.

Eggplant

Eggplant can be round, oblong or elongated. Fresh eggplants should be firm to the touch and have glossy skin. Prior to cooking, many cover eggplant slices with coarse salt to make them lose some of their bitter liquid; others, however, maintain that the distinct tangy bitterness is the main feature of this vegetable and hence must not be purged.

Bell peppers

Green peppers have a bitter and pungent flavor, yellow peppers are sweet and smooth, while the red ones are more fragrant and aromatic. Bell peppers are delicious raw, thinly sliced in mixed salads or marinated as hors d'oeuvres. If prepared this way, however, they can be hard to digest: to avoid this problem remove the skin after charring the peppers.

Tomatoes

Tomatoes are extremely versatile and, therefore, are one of the most widely used vegetables in kitchens. Knives with a serrated edge are ideal for slicing tomatoes. To remove their skins, blanch them for a few seconds in boiling water, leaving the green slem intact to prevent water from infiltrating into the fruit; after, gently squeeze them to remove excessive moisture. Tomatoes can be eaten raw or stuffed and are an excellent base for any kind of sauce.

Celery

Celery is a herbaceous plant with a strong, aromatic flavor. Celery may be either white or green, depending on the variety. White celery is usually eaten raw in crudités and mixed salads or as a hors d'oeuvre, cut into small pieces and filled with cheese. Green celery, instead, is mainly used as an aromatic vegetable. To clean celery, remove the fibrous strings from the outer stalks.

Zucchini

Zucchini can be eaten raw, thinly sliced and added to salads. But if you prefer to cook them, choose fast cooking methods which leave the flesh crisp, firm and not mushy. Zucchini are also excellent baked, fried and sautéed. Clean zucchini by washing them and removing their tips. When selecting zucchini choose the smaller ones, with a glossy skin and firm flesh, an important indicator of freshness.

AUTUMN

Beets

Beets are round or elongated red roots, rich in dietary minerals, with a sweet flavor. They can be baked, boiled or eaten raw in salads.

Mushrooms

Though mushrooms have little nutritional value, they are extremely tasty and are used extensively in food preparation to create and give flavor to a number of dishes. Some varieties (Caesar and Porcini mushrooms) can be eaten raw in salads, simply tossed in a little oil, pepper and lemon juice. Dried mushrooms are commonly available and used to give flavor to first courses and meat dishes. Mushrooms should not be washed, and any dirt should be removed with a brush or with a damp cloth.

Curly endive

Sweet and aromatic, curly endive is appreciated for its diuretic and anti-cancer properties; rich in vitamin A, it is usually eaten in salads.

Leeks

Leeks have a similar flavor to onions, though they are milder and more aromatic. They are usually used to add flavor to recipes, but can also feature as main ingredients of soups and timbales. Clean leeks by removing the bottom, more open end and the outer layers, then split in two parts and rinse the leaves under running water.

Pumpkins

Pumpkins have a sweet and aromatic flesh. The diuretic and anti-cancer properties, as well as the high content of vitamin A, make this vegetable a favorite. It can be used to prepare sauces, purées, timbales and savory pies. The flesh of a ripe pumpkin is sweet. Whole pumpkins can be stored for weeks, but once they have been cut open they should be used within a few days as they will go limp rather quickly.

WINTER

Artichokes

There are two main types of artichokes: with or without thorns. The part of the vegetable which is usually eaten is the fleshy and tasty flower bud, which can be prepared in many different ways. To prepare artichokes it is necessary to remove the outer petals and the thorny tips, as well as the "choke", a fuzzy growth covering the heart of the artichoke. To prevent cut artichokes from turning brown, place them in some water and lemon juice until ready to cook. They are excellent raw, chargrilled, stuffed, stewed and fried.

Cardoons

Cardoons belong to the same family as artichokes and share the same detoxifying properties. They can be cooked au gratin, in vegetable soups and in crudités. The outer parts must be stripped away from the central stem, which should be washed thoroughly and deprived of any fibrous strings. Once cut, cardoons darken rather quickly unless sprinkled with lemon juice.

Cabbages

This term refers to a number of vegetables of different shapes that share the same nutrients. Cabbages can be consumed either raw or cooked. A good quality cabbage should have a firm and dense head. Clean cabbages by removing and discarding the inner core and the tough outer leaves, slicing the head into thin slivers which should be rinsed under running water.

Fennels

Fennel has a crunchy texture and an aniseed-like flavor; it is high in fiber and has detoxifying properties. Fennel, preferably the rounded variety, is eaten raw, in crudités or salads. It can also be cooked, boiled or baked au gratin, and in this case any variety of fennel can be used. Fennel is best consumed when fresh, with a bright green hue and a crunchy texture. To clean fennel, remove the green, so-called "feathery" part, the outer skin and the core at the bulb's base.

Endive

Endive is a type of chicory with long white-yellowish leaves and an oval, elongated head. Endive can be eaten raw in crudités or savored in mixed salads with creamy cheeses.

Potatoes

Potato flesh has a high starch content, as well as being rich in dietary minerals and vitamins. The best way to bring out the flavor of potatoes is to steam-cook or bake them with just a minimum amount of fat. Gastronomically speaking, some distinctions can be made: potatoes with yellow flesh are firmer and best used for salads and frying; white-fleshed potatoes, on the other hand, have a floury texture and are excellent for mashing and other dishes that require a longer cooking time; new potatoes are excellent roasted or cooked in a pan. There are also red-skinned varieties. Once peeled and cut, potatoes should be kept in cold water if not cooked immediately. Potatoes keep longer if stored in a cool dark place.

Spinach

Spinach, a vegetable with shiny and crisp leaves, has a high content of vitamin A, C and iron. There are winter varieties, which are more common, and spring ones, with tender leaves, which are excellent when tossed with some oil and lemon in salads. They are one of the most frequently used vegetables, not only for their flavor but because they are easy to freeze. Spinach can be boiled, stewed or sautéed with butter, though it is best to steam-cook this vegetable to preserve all its important nutrients.

Radicchio

A peculiarity of radicchio lies in its cultivation,

based on a "forcing" method, which leads to the formation of so-called "grumoli", bunches of compacted leaves. There are a number of varieties, the most famous being the "Rosso Verona", the "Rosso Treviso" and the "Variegata Chioggia". Radicchio is eaten in salads and crudités, but it is also relished grilled and in recipes to which it confers its distinctive bitterish taste. Furthermore, it is excellent when added to timbales, soufflés and savory pies. When cleaning radicchio, the roots should be completely discarded as they are the bitterest part of this vegetable.

Escarole

Escarole, like endive, belongs to the chicory family. It has an open head and jagged leaves and is widely used in recipes belonging to central and southern Italy. It can be eaten cooked in soups, or raw in salads. It can also be used as a vegetarian filling for fresh pasta. When cleaning escarole do not remove the entire base of the head, as this part of the vegetable confers its peculiar taste.

CUTTING, CARVING AND DECORATING

There are countless ways to cut and carve vegetables. Here we show you the most common basic techniques, which can be used for everyday cooking, along with some fun decorations to add some sparkle to your dishes.

Generally speaking, depending on the degree of difficulty, there are three different ways to cut food.

• The first method is for all regular slices,

rounds and rings. It is important to check that the vegetable slices are all of a similar size to avoid significant differences in the vegetables' cooking times. The following is a variation of the common rounds. Peel some vertical strips with a zester on the vegetable's skin: this will form alternate strips of different depths. Then slice the vegetables into horizontal rounds.

• From the second group of cutting methods we can produce sticks, matchsticks and julienne, all of which differ because of their thickness. The Julienne cut described below is the thinnest. Clean the vegetables by removing the greenest parts, then cut into 2 in (5-6 cm) long pieces. Slice each piece in half lengthwise. Place the flat part of the vegetables on a cutting board and slice the vegetables lengthways into thin strips with a kitchen knife. For a better result, instead of a knife use a vegetable shredder or a special type of vegetable slicer called "mandolin slicer", with an irregular blade that gives thin matchsticks. When cooking thinly shredded vegetables, the cooking time should be reduced because you can easily overcook the vegetables, spoiling them.

•The final and most complex method is dicing, which produces medium-sized cubes. Cut the vegetables into cubes approx. ¼ in (5-7 mm) thick, peel them and slice them lengthwise into medium-thick slices. Cut the slices into matchsticks, gather them and layer them. Hold the layers with one hand and dice with a knife. If the pieces are smaller than 0.2 in (5 mm) they are known as "brunoise", cubes if they are bigger.

COOKING TECHNIQUES

Scalding /blanching

The cleaned vegetables are plunged into boiling water (hence the term "to scald") for a few seconds or up to 2 minutes. After, the vegetables are drained and placed in ice-cold water. This cooking method is suitable for delicate vegetables like snow peas. It can also be used to pre-treat vegetables before freezing, frying or peeling processes. The thermal shock brought on by scalding interrupts certain processes, like variations of color and flavor, which are inevitably caused by normal cooking procedures.

Boiling

Cooking food in abundant boiling water ensures a steady heat distribution and, therefore, an even cooking process. This is a great advantage with broccoli, for example: the flower heads do not break, the tough stalks cook rapidly and the intense green color does not fade.

Steam and pressure cooking

Steam-cooking is acceptable for all vegetables, apart from green ones which tend to loose color. A pressure cooker is a very fast way to prepare food: it halves cooking times and ensures an excellent outcome.

The following steps ensure the best results in steam-cooking:
•Pour approx. 2 cups of cold water on the bottom of a pot. Stainless steel pots are a better option.
•Place the vegetables in the opposite steam basket. If you do not have a basket, place the vegetables in a steel colander that fits into the pot.
•Vegetables that have the same cooking time can be cooked together. Place the basket on the pot and place on a stove. Cook the vegetables over medium heat, covering the pot with a lid.

If a pressure cooker is used, cover the vegetables with some cold water. Make sure that the lid is well sealed. Calculate cooking time from when the pot starts to whistle. Then, release the steam

through the valve before opening the pressure cooker.

Poaching

This cooking method is best for certain types of vegetables, like carrots and celery root, which can be cut into small pieces.

Even spinach can be cooked this way, as it does not require much water to cook. If water is replaced with some broth or stock, the condensed liquid can be used as a delicious sauce.

There is just one inconvenience: if there are a lot of ingredients, they may not cook evenly.

Here is how to cook carrots:
•Peel and dice carrots and boil in a little water in a pan with a lid (the water should just cover the vegetables).
•When the water starts to boil, leave to simmer on a low flame until the vegetables are cooked.

HOW TO PREPARE VEGETABLE STOCK

Ingredients for 4 cups (1,5 l)
2 medium-sized onions
½ cup (100 g) broccoli stalks
1 medium (200 g) leek
⅔ lb (300 g) carrots
¼ lb (200 g) celery
⅓ lb (150 g) zucchini
2 Tbsp (20 g) extra virgin olive oil
1 cup (250 ml) white wine
12 cups (3 l) water
½ grilled onion (or lightly toasted in a pan)
1 thyme sprig
1 rosemary sprig
1 bay leaf
½ garlic clove
1 clove

1. Peel the onions and slice into big rings. Rinse all the vegetables and cut into small pieces.

2. Sauté the onion in some oil with 1 tablespoon water. Add the vegetables and quickly stir fry in an open pan. Pour the wine and leave to evaporate, then add some water.

3. Add ½ an onion and the herbs, mix and leave to simmer on medium heat for 30-40 minutes; every now and again skim off any foam that rises to the surface.

4. Filter the stock through cheesecloth and gather the liquid in a pot. Leave to boil until the liquid has reduced to 4 ½ cups.

Vegetables **en Croute**

Asparagus Loaf
in a Crisp Pastry Shell

Serves 4

For the loaf:
²/₃ lb (250 g) pate brisée
8 large asparagus
1 ½ cup (180 g) all-purpose flour
3 eggs
²/₃ (100 ml) milk
½ cup (100 g) soft goat cheese
6 Tbsp extra-virgin olive oil
1 packet yeast
2 Tbsp gruyère cheese
1 pat butter
salt and pepper

Grease and dust the ovenproof dish with flour; line with the pate brisée and bake in oven at 375°F (190°C) for 12 minutes.

1. Lightly peel and remove the toughest parts of the asparagus and boil in salted water (Picture 1).

2. Whisk the eggs in a bowl with the milk, salt and pepper. Add the sifted flour and yeast, slowly drizzle with the extra-virgin olive oil and add the goat cheese. Add the grated gruyère cheese and fill the pastry-lined ovenproof dish, alternating layers of this mixture and the asparagus.

3. Bake at 350°F (180°C) for approx. 45 minutes. Leave to cool and unmold. Serve the loaf warm.

Kitchen tip The asparagus can be replaced with other vegetables such as zucchini, peas, string beans or snow peas or some combination of them all.

Preparation time 30 minutes
Cooking time 50 minutes
Difficulty Easy
Calories 427
Wine Alto Adige Gewürztraminer

Pumpkin, Cheese
and Truffle Cannelloni

Serves 6

For the cannelloni:
1 packet of pasta sheets

For the filling:
½ green round pumpkin
1 ½ cup (150 g) quartirolo cheese
4 Tbsp (20 g) black truffle
2-3 drops truffle oil
4 Tbsp grated parmesan cheese
2 pats butter
1 thyme sprig
salt and pepper

Preparation time 30 minutes
Cooking time 50 minutes
Difficulty Medium
Calories 302
Wine Valle Isarco Gewürztraminer

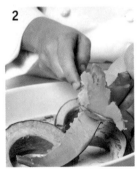

Cut the pumpkin into slices ¾ to 1-¼ inch (2-3 cm) thick and, without removing the rind, place in a casserole dish lined with non-stick oven paper. Sprinkle with salt and water (Picture 1) and bake at 350°F (180°C) for 25-30 minutes.

1. Remove the flesh from the pumpkin rind with a tablespoon (Picture 2) and pass it through a food processor; place in a bowl.

2. Crumble the quartirolo and add it to the pumpkin flesh (Picture 3), together with the grated parmesan, the truffle oil and the thyme leaves. Add salt and pepper to taste and put aside.

3. Chop the black truffle finely and lightly fry it in some butter. Divide the layers of pastry and brush each one with some melted butter. Place two layers on top of each other and, with the aid of a piping bag, put some filling on one side of the pastry.

4. Roll the pastry to form some small rolls (Picture 4), seal the sides and brush the surface with the melted butter. Bake in a hot oven at 350°F (180°C) for 20-25 minutes. Serve the cannelloni hot or warm.

Kitchen tip The pasta sheets can be purchased in Chinese food stores, or they can be replaced with the more common fillo pastry.

Porcini Mushrooms
and Asiago Cheese en Croute

Serves 4

For the pastry:
⅔ lb (250 g) puff pastry

For the filling:
1 ¾ lb (180 g) asiago cheese
½ lb (250 g) porcini mushrooms
2 Tbsp extra-virgin olive oil
1 shallot
parsley
½ chili pepper
salt and pepper

Cut the cheese into small pieces and put aside. Clean the porcini with damp paper towels and scrape off the dirt; chop up the stems (Picture 1) and thinly slice the heads (Picture 2).

1. Warm the chopped shallot with the oil in a non-stick pan; add the crumbled chili pepper and mushrooms. Sauté on a high flame and dust with chopped parsley, salt and pepper.

2. Roll out the puff pastry on a pie tin lined with non-stick oven paper and sprinkle the cheese on one half. Add the mushrooms and fold over the other half to cover. Finally, seal the edges by pressing firmly, and prick some holes in the pastry with a fork.

3. Bake in the oven at 400°F (200°C) for approx. 25 minutes and serve warm.

Kitchen tip The puff pastry can be used to make stuffed savory croissants. After rolling out the pastry, divide it into 8 equal triangles. Brush the tip and bottom of each pastry triangle with the beaten egg. Put 1 tablespoon of filling on the tip of the triangles and roll them up, starting from the bottom end. Press the edges and curve them towards the center. Bake in oven at 400°F (200°C) for approx. 15 minutes.

Preparation time 10 minutes
Cooking time 30 minutes
Difficulty Easy
Calories 451
Wine Cabernet di Breganze

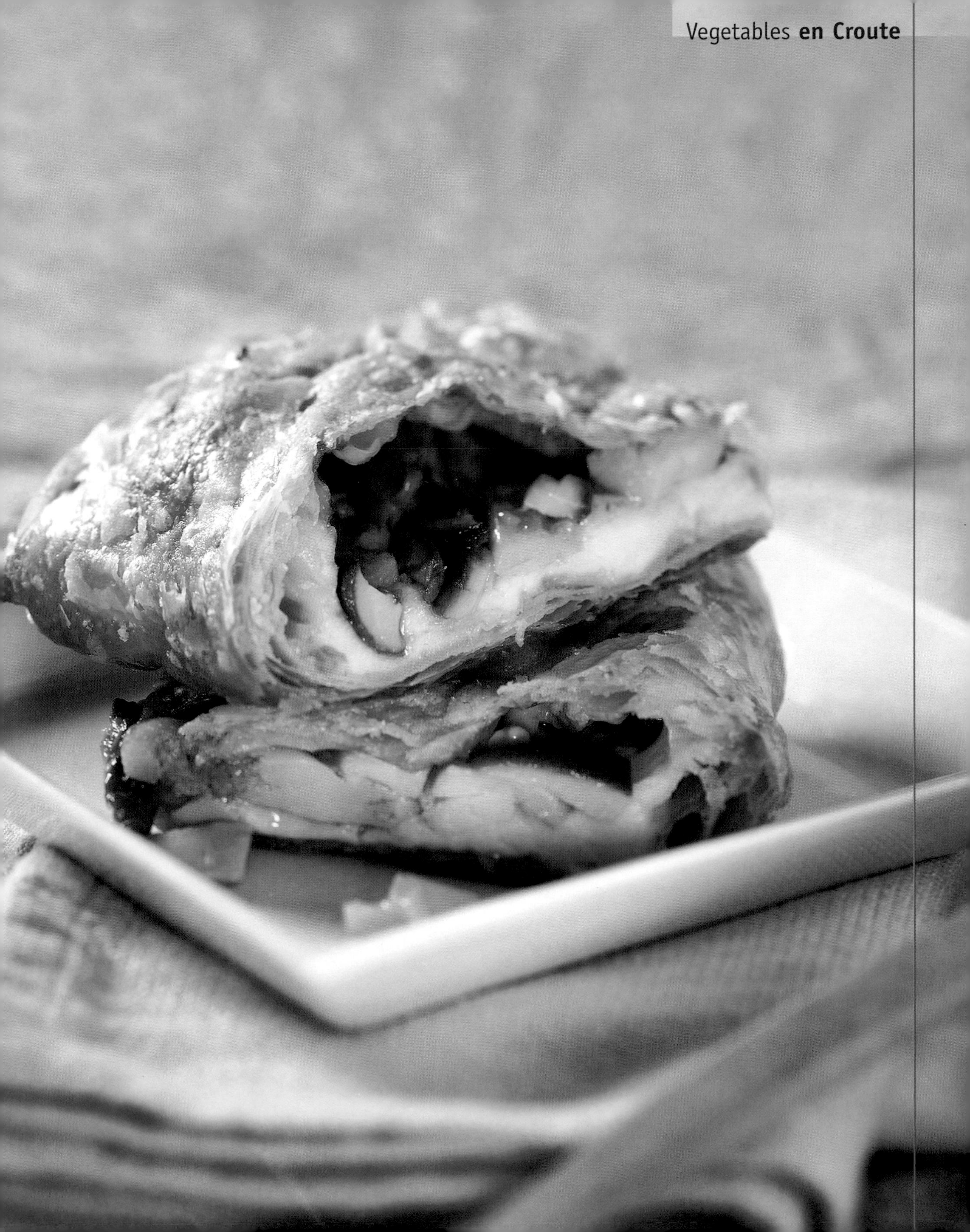

Summer Vegetable
Pastry

Serves 4

For the pastry shell:

1 ¼ lb (400 g) pate brisée
(see recipe p. 28)

⅔ lb (300 g) eggplant

⅔ lb (300 g) zucchini

¼ lb (125g) yellow bell peppers

¼ lb (125g) red bell peppers

3 round red tomatoes

¾ lb (350 g) scamorza cheese

6 Tbsp extra-virgin olive oil

salt and pepper

Preparation time 35 minutes
Cooking time 45 minutes
Difficulty Medium
Calories 785
Wine Verdiso

Peel the eggplant and slice into rounds of approx. ¼ in (5 mm). Fry for 2 minutes in 4 Tbsp of oil; drain and leave to cool slightly.

1. Clean the zucchini and slice into rounds: fry lightly in another pan for 3-4 minutes and season to taste. Grill the bell peppers, cool them in cold water, peel and cut them into strips. Toss the bell peppers in a couple of Tbsp of oil, salt and pepper.

2. Clean the tomatoes, cut them into thin wedges and dress them with the remaining oil and some salt. Thinly slice the scamorza and put aside.

3. Line a pie pan which has been previously greased and dusted with flour with the thinly rolled-out pate brisée. Add the eggplant, zucchini (Picture 1), sliced scamorza (Picture 2), strips of bell peppers (Picture 3) and tomatoes. Make another layer of vegetables and place a pastry lid the size of the pan over the filling (Picture 4).

4. Trim away excess pastry from the edges and, folding the pastry towards the center of the pie, seal the edges. Set the oven at 350°F (180°C). Prick the pastry and, when the oven is hot, bake for 30 minutes. Serve the pastry hot.

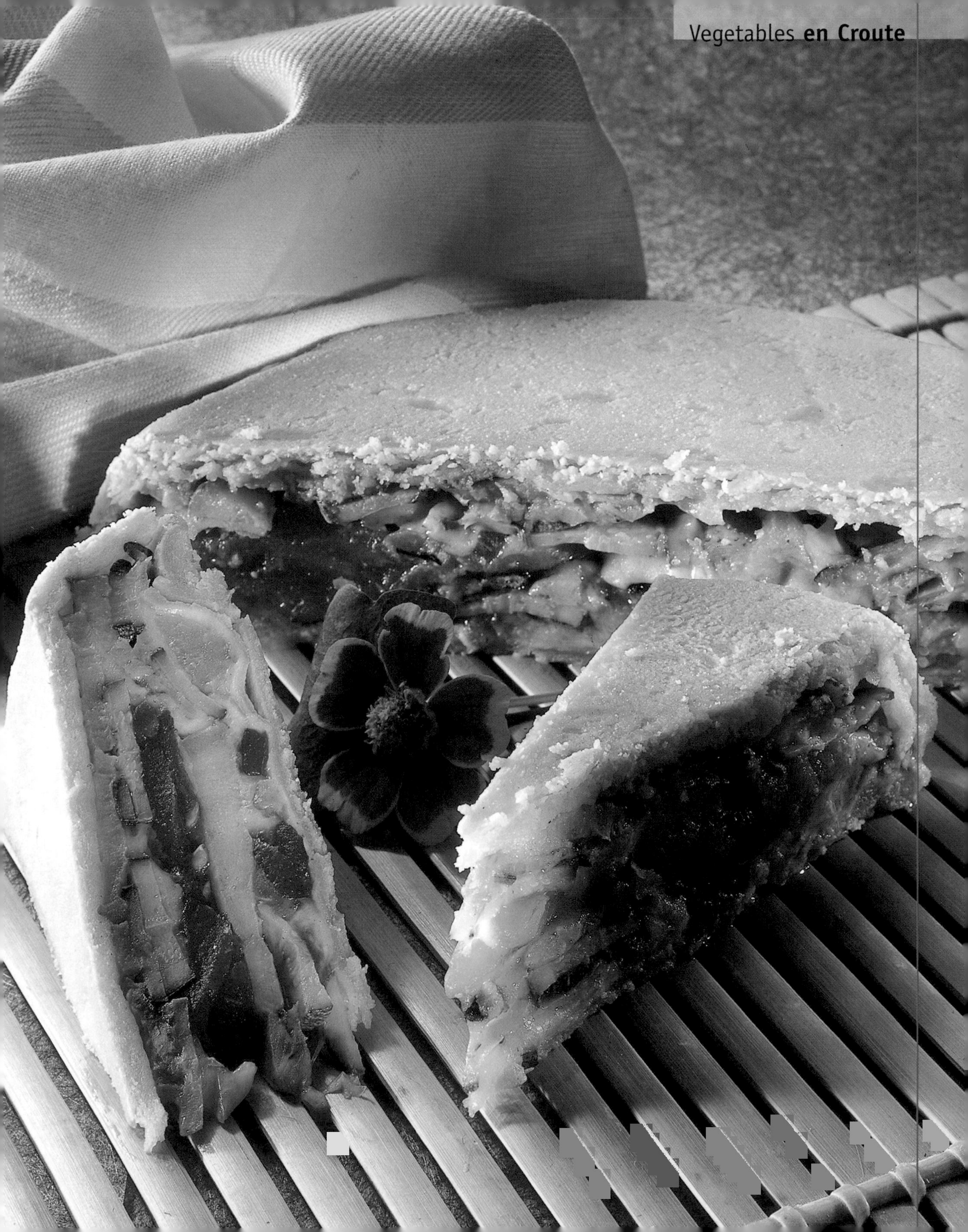

Mini Potato Focaccia Rolls
with Grilled Vegetables

Serves 4

For the focaccia rolls:
2 cups (250 g) all-purpose flour
¼ lb (120 g) potatoes
⅔ cup (100 ml) milk
½ packet brewer's yeast
2 Tbsp extra-virgin olive oil

For the vegetables:
⅔ cup (150 g) eggplant and
   zucchini in oil
⅓ lb (150 g) cherry tomatoes
⅓ lb (150 g) buffalo-mozzarella
oregano
salt and pepper

Melt the yeast in the milk and add the flour and oil. Boil and mash the potatoes, add to the yeast mixture and work to a smooth dough (Picture 1).

1. Form a ball, cover with a cloth and leave to rise for approx 1 hour.

2. Place the tomatoes on a baking tray, brush them with some oil and season with salt, pepper and oregano. Bake in the oven at 350°F (180°C) for 15 minutes. Cut the mozzarella into small pieces and leave to dry on some kitchen paper.

3. Roll out the dough and divide into small cylinders (Picture 2), cut them into pieces and form some small circles about 3 in (8 cm) in diameter; place them on a baking tray and leave to rise for another 15 minutes. Bake at 375°F (190°C) for 15 minutes.

4. Spread some vegetables and mozzarella on every focaccia roll and place in the oven for another 5 minutes. Serve hot.

Kitchen tip Vary the flavor of your focaccia rolls by replacing the vegetables with button mushrooms and thinly sliced fresh zucchini. Before serving, brush the mushrooms and zucchini with olive oil, add salt and then arrange on the dough.

Preparation time 15 minutes
Cooking time 20 minutes
Difficulty Easy
Calories 405
Wine Orvieto Classico

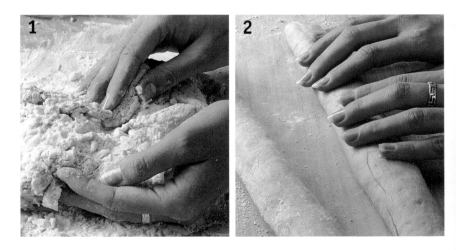

Endive
and Leek Pie

Serves 6

For the pate brisée:
1 cup (125 g) all-purpose flour
2 ¼ sticks (250 g) butter
1 egg
2 yolks
3 Tbsp white wine
salt

For the filling:
1 cup (250 ml) béchamel sauce
1 egg
¾ lb (350 g) endive
½ leek
1 tsp sugar
3 Tbsp extra-virgin olive oil
5 Tbsp grated parmesan
1 small bunch of chives
salt and pepper

Preparation time 45 minutes
Cooking time 45 minutes
Difficulty Medium
Calories 550
Wine Colli Piacentini Sauvignon

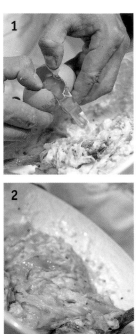

Make a well with the flour, break 1 egg into the center and add the butter, 1 egg yolk, the wine and some salt. Knead until the pastry is consistent, then place it in a bag and let dough rest in the refrigerator for 30 minutes.

1. Clean the endive and cut it into strips. Wash the leek and slice it into rounds. Sauté the leek in a pan with the oil, add the endive and fry lightly for 4-5 minutes. Add sugar, salt and pepper to taste and cook for another 10 minutes.

2. Pour the endive in a bowl, add 1 egg (Pictures 1-2), the parmesan, the shredded chives and béchamel sauce (Picture 3) and stir until well blended (Picture 4).

3. Divide the pastry into 2 parts and roll out into a sheet about ¼ in (5 mm) thick. Grease a pie pan, dust with flour and line the bottom and edges with one of the rolled out sheets of pate brisée. Pour the endive filling on the dough, brush the edges with some egg yolk and close with the remaining pate brisée.

4. Brush the top of the pastry with the egg yolk and bake in oven at 350°F (180°C) for 30 minutes; serve the pie hot.

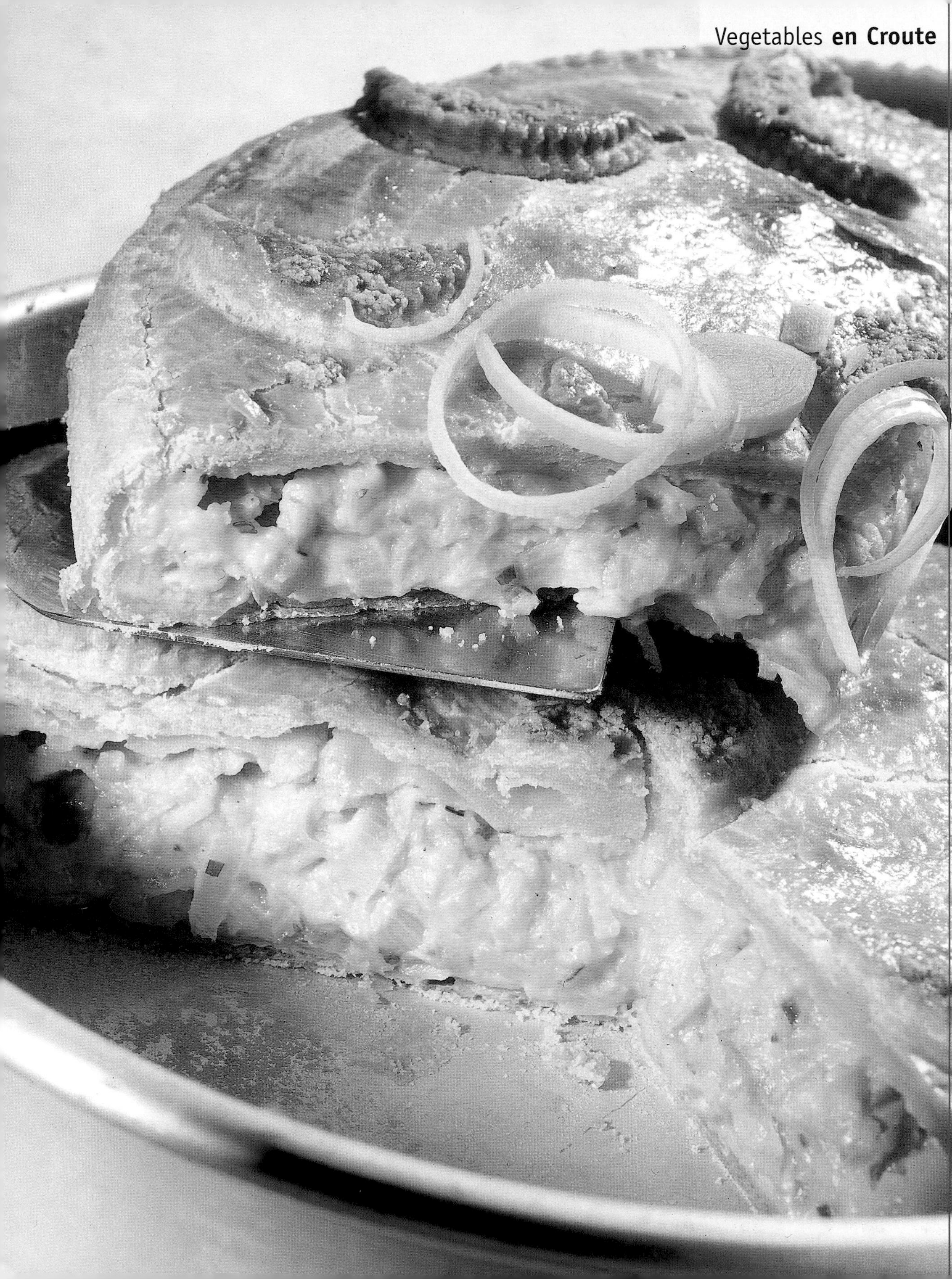

Artichoke
and Smoked Trout Tart

Serves 4

For the pastry:
2 ½ cups (300 g) all-purpose flour
6 Tbsp extra-virgin olive oil
salt

For the filling:
1 lb (500 g) artichokes
½ lb (200 g) smoked trout
2 cloves garlic
4 ½ cups (1 l) vegetable broth
1 ½ pats butter
4 Tbsp (30 g) all-purpose flour
1 marjoram sprig
1 lemon
salt and pepper

Preparation time 40 minutes
Cooking time 45 minutes
Difficulty Medium
Calories 607
Wine Lugana

Prepare the pastry with the flour, the oil and a pinch of salt, adding enough water to obtain a smooth dough (Picture 1). Form a ball, cover and leave to rest for 20 minutes.

1. Clean the artichokes and place the hearts in some water and lemon juice. Blanch the artichokes for 7-8 minutes in the boiling broth. Drain the artichokes (keep the water that the artichokes were cooked in); slice and sauté them in pan with 2 Tbsp of oil, the crushed clove garlics and the marjoram.

2. Melt the butter in a saucepan, add the flour and toast for a few minutes. Pour 1 ½ cup (300 ml) of the artichoke water and whisk. Cook for 10 minutes, stirring with a wooden spoon. Add salt and pepper to taste and put the cream aside.

3. Thinly roll out the pastry (Picture 2) and line a round ovenproof dish. Spread some sliced artichokes on the bottom, continue with some pieces of smoked trout and repeat until finished. Cover with the previously prepared cream, finish with a pastry lattice topping and bake at 350°F (180°C) for 25 minutes. Serve the pie either warm or cold.

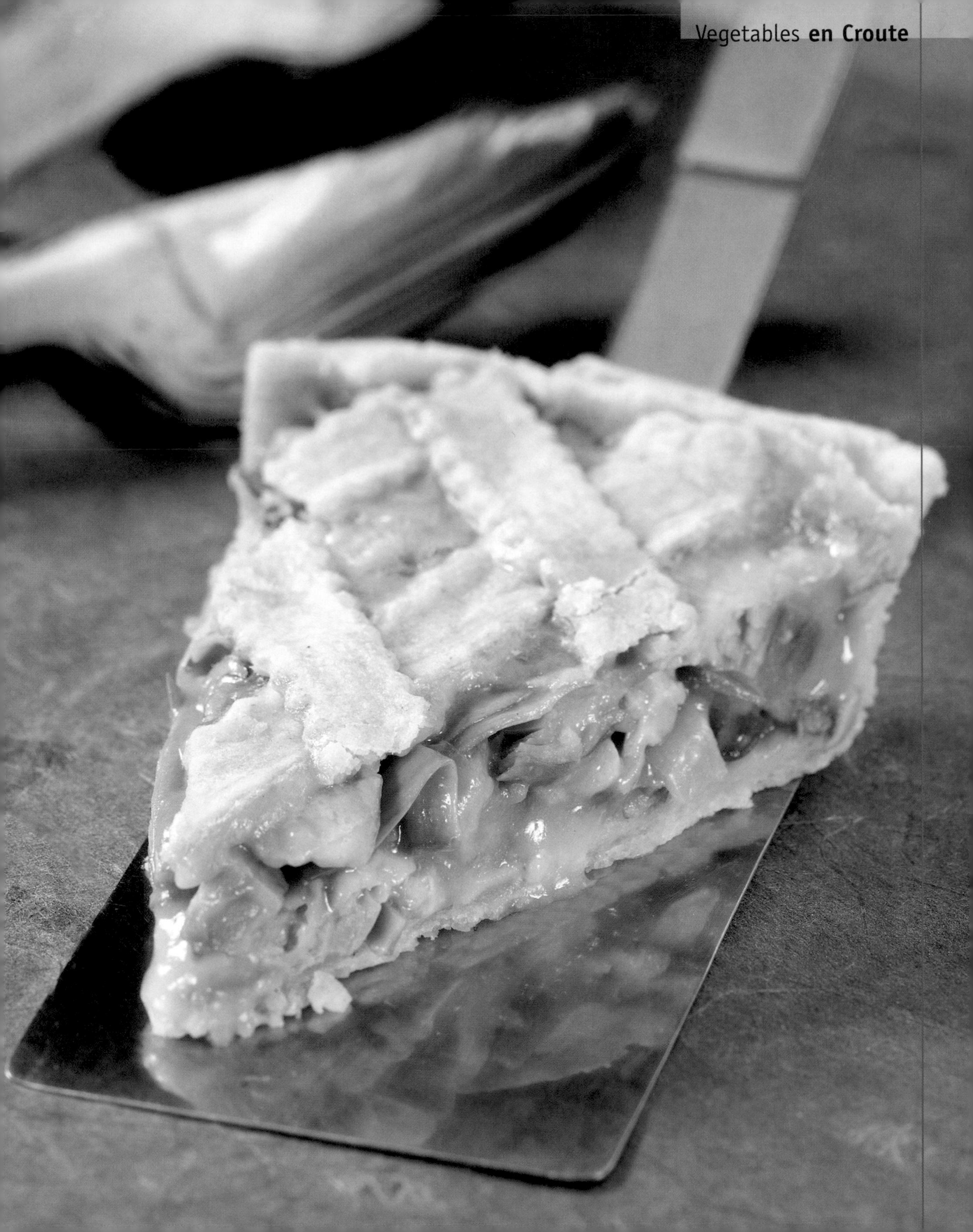

Carrot Pie
with Bagòss Cheese Fondue

Serves 8

For the pastry shell:
⅔ lb (250 g) puff pastry

For the filling:
1 ¼ lb (600 g) carrots
⅔ cup (100 ml) fresh cream
3 Tbsp grated parmesan
1 pat butter
2 eggs
1 thyme sprig
2 Tbsp extra-virgin olive oil
1 grating of nutmeg
salt and pepper

For the fondue:
1 ⅓ cup (300 ml) milk
¼ lb (80 g) bagòss cheese
4 Tbsp (30 g) all-purpose flour
2 pats butter
1 egg yolk
nutmeg
salt and pepper

Preparation time 1 hour
Cooking time 1 hour
Difficulty Medium
Calories 405
Wine Nebbiolo d'Alba

Peel the carrots, keep 2 aside and slice the others into rounds. Cook in a saucepan with 2 Tbsp of oil, a pinch of salt and ½ cup of water. When they are soft and dry, blend in a food processor until smooth and leave to cool.

1. Add the parmesan, eggs, cream, salt, pepper and nutmeg to the carrots and stir until well blended.

2. Line a 9 in (24 cm) diameter pie dish with the puff pastry, pour in the mixture and bake at 350°F (180°C) for 35-40 minutes.

3. Slice the 2 carrots kept aside into diagonal rounds and blanch in salted water for 2-3 minutes. Melt the butter in a pan, add the carrots and sauté for 2 minutes. Add the thyme leafs, salt and pepper.

4. Melt the butter in a saucepan, add the flour (Picture 1) and warm milk stirring constantly with a whisk (Picture 2). Five minutes after boiling begins, add the pieces of bagòss cheese (Picture 3).

5. When the cheese has completely melted and is well blended, remove the saucepan from heat and add 1 egg yolk. Season with salt and pepper and dust with nutmeg (Picture 4).

6. Distribute the carrot rounds on the pie and serve the slices with the fondue.

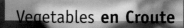

Vegetable and Cheese
Roll

Serves 6

For the roll:
²/₃ lb (250 g) puff pastry

For the filling:
½ lb (250 g) frozen spinach
¼ lb (120 g) carrots
⅓ lb (150 g) potatoes
¾ cup (80 g) peas
1 ½ lb (150 g) meltable cheese
½ cup (120 ml) cooking cream
2 pats butter
nutmeg
salt and pepper

Clean the potatoes and the carrots and dice into small pieces. Blanch the diced vegetables and the peas in a saucepan of lightly salted boiling water for 3-4 minutes.

1. Melt the butter in a pan and add the boiled vegetables (Picture 1) and the defrosted, drained and finely chopped spinach. Cook for 4-5 minutes, add salt and pepper.

2. Add a pinch of nutmeg and the cream. Stir with a wooden spoon until well blended and continue to cook until the cream thickens and merges with the vegetables. Remove from heat and leave to cool.

3. Roll out the puff pastry and cover it with the slices of meltable cheese (Picture 2). Spread the vegetables on the cheese. Roll up the pastry with the vegetable filling inside (Picture 3) and press the edges firmly to seal in the filling. Brush the surface of the pastry with the beaten egg.

4. Gently place the vegetable roll on a baking tray, either lightly greased or lined with a sheet of non-stick oven paper, making sure the roll doesn't break. Bake in a hot oven at 350°F (180°C) for approx. 40 minutes. Once cooked, remove the roll from the oven, leave to cool, slice and serve.

Preparation time 30 minutes
Cooking time 50 minutes
Difficulty Easy
Calories 374
Wine Cirò Bianco

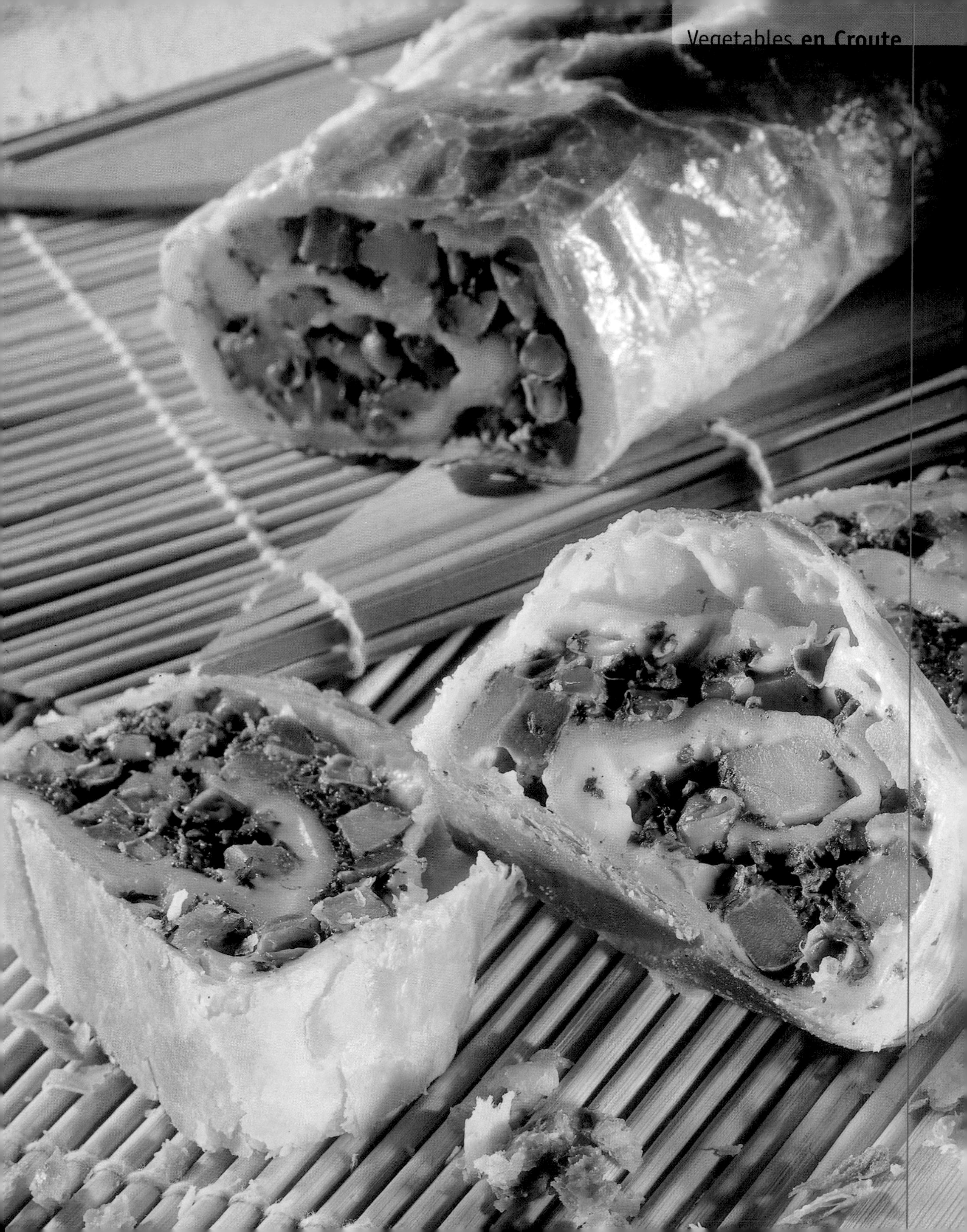

Puff Pastry Baskets
with Stewed Vegetables

Serves 6

For the baskets:
²/₃ lb (250 g) puff pastry
salt

For the vegetables:
¹/₃ lb (120 g) zucchini
¼ lb (100 g) asparagus spears
¾ lb (150 g) carrots
¾ lb (150 g) potatoes
¼ lb (100 g) artichokes
¼ lb (80 g) green onions
1 clove garlic
3 Tbsp extra-virgin olive oil
¼ lb (80 g) emmental cheese
chives
salt and pepper

Roll out the puff pastry on a lightly floured surface into an approx. ¼ in (3-4 mm)-thick sheet.

1. Cut the pastry into 6 in (15 cm) diameter circles (Picture 1). Line some 5 in (12-13 cm) muffin cups with the puff pastry circles, pressing the pastry lightly along the edges (Picture 2). Sprinkle a pinch of salt over every cup.

2. Prick the pastry with a fork so that it stays flat during baking. Place in oven and bake for 12 minutes at 375°F (190°C).

3. Clean the vegetables: trim and cut the zucchini, the carrots and the potatoes into triangles or crescents about ¼ in (½ cm) thick. Cut the asparagus into ¾ in (2 cm)-thick rounds, leaving the tips whole. Clean the artichokes and cut into thin slices. Clean the onion and slice into rounds. Peel the clove of garlic, add to the other vegetables and boil for 3 minutes in salted water. Drain and discard the garlic.

4. Warm the oil in a pan and sauté the vegetables for 3 minutes (Picture 3); add salt and pepper and dust with the chopped chives. Add the diced Emmental and mix in with the vegetables. Fill the baskets with this mixture and serve.

Preparation time 25 minutes
Cooking time 20 minutes
Difficulty Medium
Calories 262
Wine Alto Adige Pinot Grigio

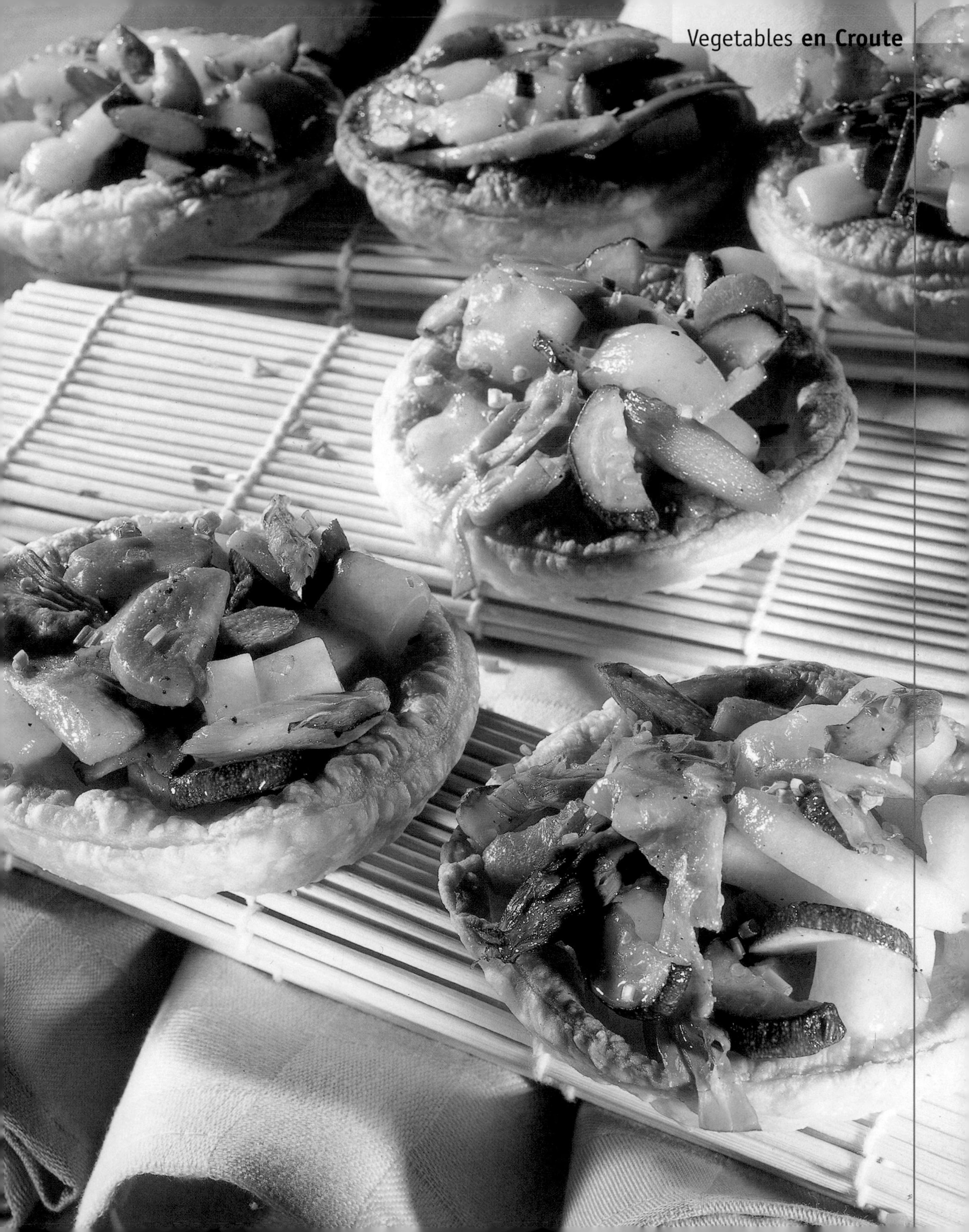

Winter Vegetable
Quiche

Serves 4

For the pastry shell:
²/₃ lb (250 g) pate brisée

For the filling:
¼ yellow pumpkin
½ Savoy cabbage
2 carrots
1 yellow onion
½ yellow bell pepper
1 slice cooked ham
½ stick (50 g) butter
2 eggs
nutmeg
salt and pepper

Preparation time 15 minutes
Cooking time 45 minutes
Difficulty Easy
Calories 375
Wine Trentino Marzemino

Remove the rind (Picture 1) and the seeds from the pumpkin and dice (Picture 2). Finely slice the onion and gently cook it in the saucepan with the butter. Add the pumpkin and the diced bell pepper; cook covered on a low flame for 5 minutes.

1. In the meantime, peel the carrots, cut them into small pieces and add them to the saucepan. Slice the Savoy cabbage and wash it in a basin in cold water, dry it properly and place in the saucepan with the other vegetables. Add salt and pepper and cook for 10 minutes. Warm the oven at 350°F (180°C).

2. Line the pie pan with the pate brisée and prick the bottom with a fork. Remove the vegetables from the stove and place in a bowl to cool; add the eggs (Picture 3), nutmeg and the ham cut into thin strips.

3. Pour the mixture into the pie pan, fold the edges of pastry towards the center of the pie and bake for 20 minutes. Serve the quiche hot.

Kitchen tip Prepare homemade pate brisée in the following way: quickly mix 2 cups (250 g) all-purpose flour with 1 stick (120 g) cold butter, 1 egg yolk, a pinch of salt and a little water. Let the dough rest in a cool place for approx. 20 minutes before use.

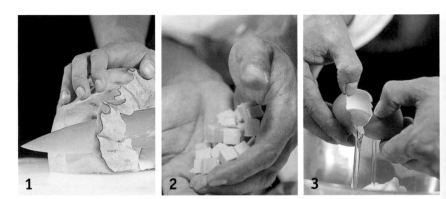

1   2   3

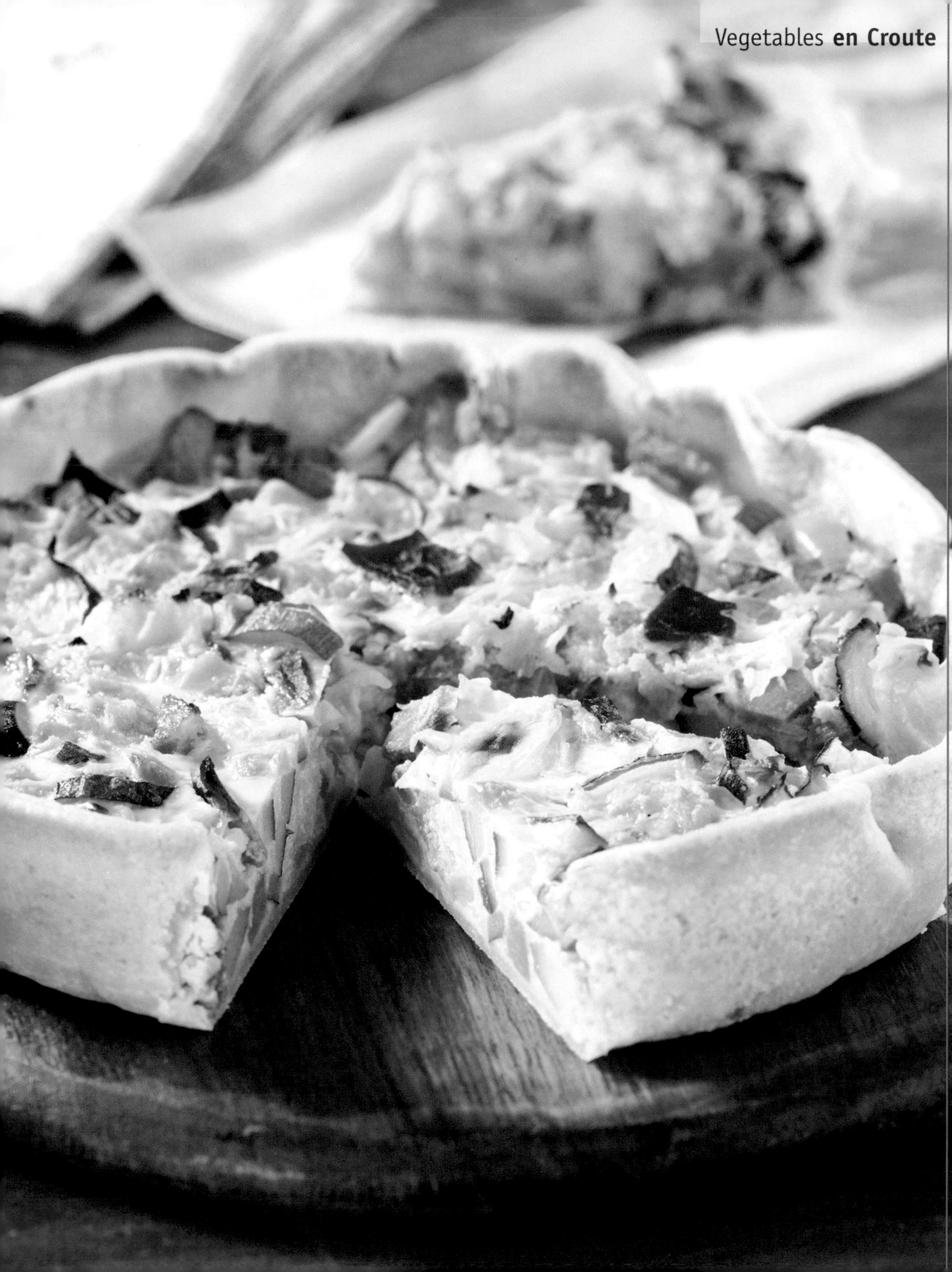

Spinach Pie
with Carrot Cream

Serves 4

For the pastry shell:
²/₃ lb (250 g) puff pastry
1 egg

For the filling:
7 Tbsp grated parmesan
½ lb (180 g) fresh spinach
1 ⅓ cup (300 g) ricotta cheese
1 egg
nutmeg
salt and pepper

For the carrot cream:
²/₃ lb (300 g) carrots
½ lb (250 g) potatoes
²/₃ lb (100 ml) fresh cream
4 cups (½ l) vegetable broth
½ onion
2 pats butter
salt and pepper

Preparation time 35 minutes
Cooking time 55 minutes
Difficulty Medium
Calories 645
Wine Terre di Franciacorta
       Bianco

Wash the spinach, cut into strips (Picture 1) and place in a bowl. Add the ricotta, the parmesan, the egg, a grating of nutmeg, salt and pepper and mix well.

1. Roll out the pastry into a ¼ in (½ cm) thick sheet. Grease a pie pan and dust with a little flour. Line the pan with the pastry and fill with the spinach and ricotta filling. Brush the edges of the pastry with some beaten egg and cover the pie with the rest of the thinly rolled pastry.

2. Brush the surface of the pie with the beaten egg. Decorate with crescents or leaves made from the leftover pastry. Bake the pie in the oven for 35 minutes at 350°F (180°C).

3. Peel, wash and chop the carrots and the potatoes and put aside. Peel and cut the onion into thin slices. Melt the butter in a saucepan; add the sliced onion and brown lightly for a few minutes over moderate heat. Add the carrots and potatoes (Picture 2) and season with salt and pepper. Cook for 5 minutes and pour in the vegetable broth. Leave to simmer on a slow fire for 15 minutes.

5. Add the cream and cook for another 5 minutes. Puree the carrots and the potatoes finely with a food processor (Picture 3). Remove the pie from the oven, cut into slices and serve with the carrot cream.

1   2

40

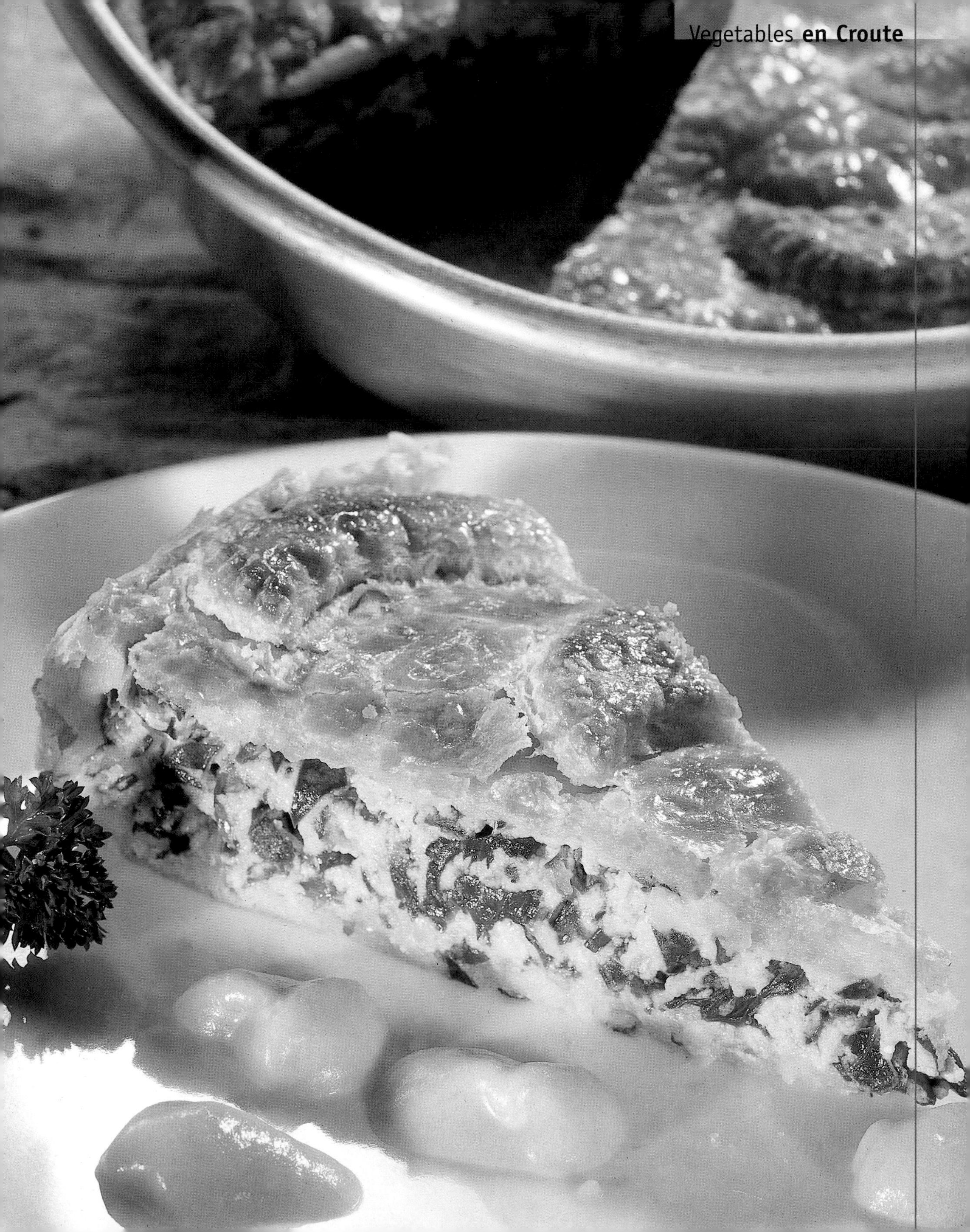

Broccoli
and Salt Cod Pie

Serves 4

For the pastry shell:
1 ⅓ lb (500 g) puff pastry

For the filling:
2 tomatoes
1 egg
1 lb (400 g) soaked salt cod
1 lb (400 g) broccoli heads
4 Tbsp extra-virgin olive oil
7 Tbsp grated parmesan
½ onion
salt and pepper

Preparation time 20 minutes
Cooking time 45 minutes
Difficulty Easy
Calories 450
Wine Friuli Vitovska

Remove and discard the skin from the salt cod (Picture 1) and break up the flesh into small flakes. Chop the onion and sauté in a pan with some oil; add the pieces salt cod and lightly fry for a few minutes.

1. Chop the tomatoes with a knife, add them to the pan with some salt and pepper and cook covered for about 15 minutes.

2. Boil the broccoli heads in boiling salted water, drain, chop coarsely and mix with the fish. Remove from heat and add the parmesan (Picture 2) and egg.

3. Line a 9 in (24 cm) diameter pie dish with some puff pastry. Pour in the mixture (Picture 3) and spread evenly. Cover the filling with the rest of the puff pastry.

4. Seal the pastry edges and brush the surface with the beaten egg (Picture 4). Prick the pastry with a skewer and bake in oven at 375°F (190°C) for 30-35 minutes or until golden. Serve the broccoli and salt cod pie hot or warm.

Kitchen tip If you don't like broccoli replace the broccoli with 2 or 3 boiled potatoes mashed with a fork.

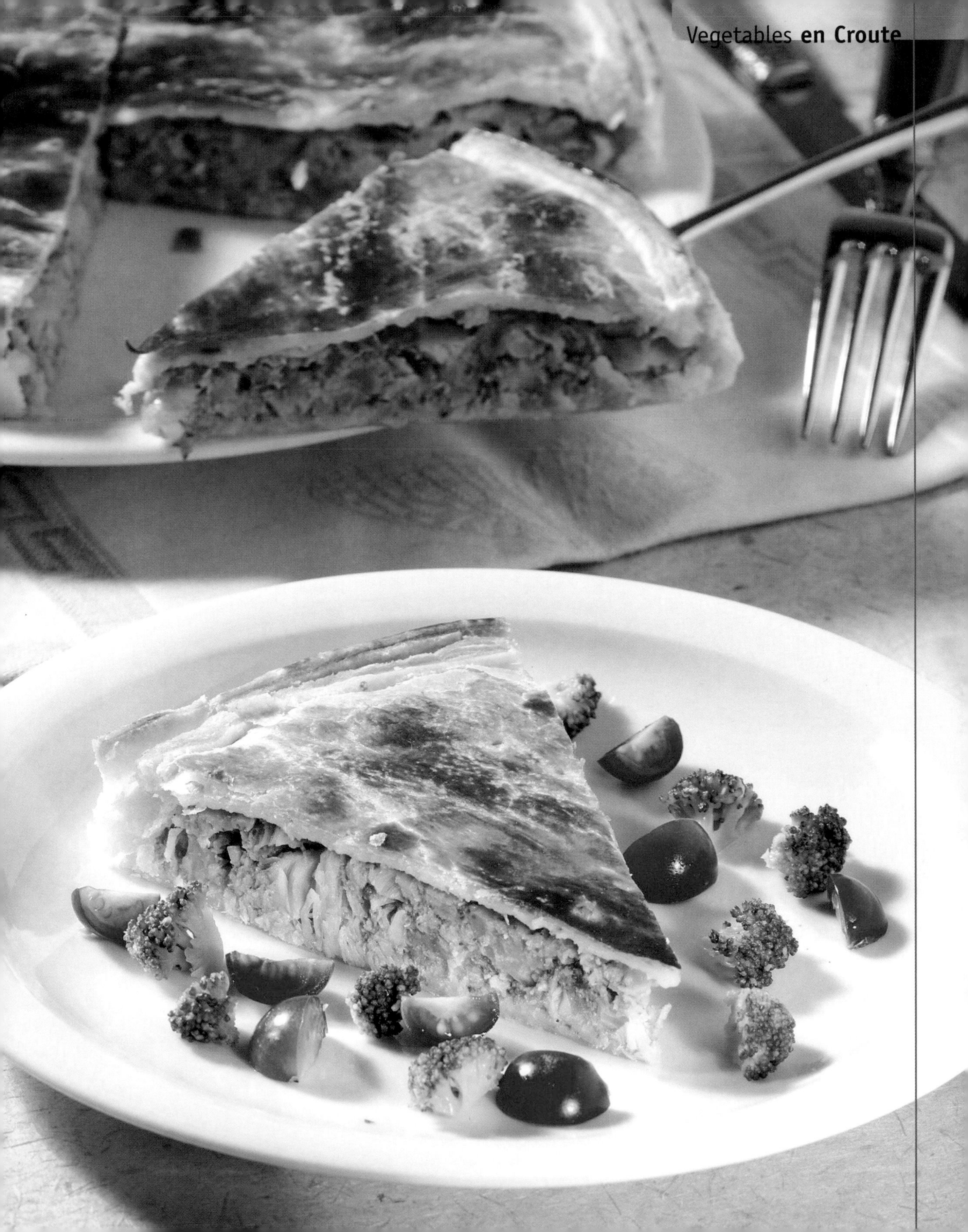

Vesuvian-Style
Strudel

Serves 4-6

For the strudel:

1 packet puff pastry
4 salted anchovy fillets
1 tsp oregano
½ lb (200 g) sweet provolone cheese
½ lb (200 g) vine tomatoes
3 Tbsp (25 g) capers
½ cup (50 g) pitted green olives
salt and pepper

Preparation time 30 minutes
Cooking time 30 minutes
Difficulty easy
Calories 310
Wine Greco di Tufo

Set the oven temperature at 375°F (190°C). Thinly roll out the puff pastry onto a lightly floured surface.

1. Cover the entire sheet of pastry with a layer of provolone slices (Picture 1). Peel the tomatoes and chop with the capers, washed and dried, the olives and the desalted anchovy fillets and scatter over the slices of cheese (Pictures 2-3).

2. Dust with oregano, roll up the pastry (Picture 4) and seal the edges carefully.

3. Place the roll on a well-greased baking tray and bake for about half an hour. Remove the strudel from the oven and leave to cool before serving.

Interesting to know Provolone was originally made in south Italy but today it is mainly produced in the areas near Cremona, Brescia and Piacenza. There are two main types of provolone: the sweet one, with a mild smell and flavor, and the piquant one, with a stronger flavor and a sharp smell.

Fried Vegetables

Fried Pumpkin
with Creamed Savoy Cabbage and Potatoes

Serves 4

For the pumpkin:
¼ green skinned pumpkin
vegetable oil

For the creamed cabbage:
2 medium potatoes
¼ Savoy cabbage
2 garlic cloves
3 Tbsp extra-virgin olive oil
1 cup (300ml) vegetable broth
  (or hot water)
chives
salt and pepper

Preparation time 20 minutes
Cooking time 15 minutes
Difficulty Easy
Calories 275
Wine Alto Adige Gewürztraminer

Peel the potatoes and slice them thinly; wash and julienne the Savoy cabbage (Picture 1).

1. Lightly fry the crushed garlic in a pan with olive oil until golden, add the Savoy cabbage and the potatoes and season with salt and pepper. After 2 minutes, cover with the hot broth and add some salt. Cook slowly until the vegetables are soft and the broth has reduced sufficiently; Puree the mixture in a processor (Picture 2) and season to taste.

2. While the creamed cabbage is cooling in the refrigerator (approx. 20 minutes), remove the green rind from the pumpkin and cut the flesh into thin strips (Picture 3).

3. Warm the vegetable oil in a pan and fry the pumpkin for 1 minute (Picture 4). Drain well on some paper towels.

4. Make some quenelles with the creamed cabbage and potatoes with the aid of 2 damp Tbsp, arrange on plates and cover with the crispy pumpkin. Dust with chives and serve.

Kitchen tip If any creamed cabbage is left over, it can be used to make a spread for toasted French bread, adding any other ingredient with an intense flavor to contrast the sweetness of the Savoy cabbage. As an alternative, add a handful of breadcrumbs and 1 egg to the creamed mixture to give it more texture; form croquettes, coat in breadcrumbs and fry.

Fried Zucchini Flowers
in Tomato Sauce

Serves 4

For the zucchini flowers:
12 zucchini flowers
1 ½ cup (200 g) self-rising flour
2 eggs
⅓ cup (100 ml) light beer
2 Tbsp extra-virgin olive oil
2 Tbsp chopped herbs
4 cups (1 l) peanut oil
salt

For the tomato sauce:
½ lb (250 g) ripe tomatoes
½ lemon
4 Tbsp extra-virgin olive oil
1 Tbsp white vinegar
2 Tbsp Worchester sauce
salt and pepper

Sift the flour, add the yolks, the extra-virgin olive oil, the herbs and beer. Mix until smooth, then cover the batter and leave to rest for approx. 1 hour.

1. Blanch the tomatoes in boiling water, peel them (Picture 1) and cut into chunks (Picture 2). Marinate the tomatoes with olive oil, Worchester sauce, lemon juice, vinegar, salt and pepper.

2. Beat the egg whites until they are stiff and fold into the batter; dip the closed zucchini flowers in the mixture and fry in very hot oil.

3. Sprinkle some salt and serve the zucchini flowers hot with some tomato sauce.

Kitchen tip To make an excellent batter in a short time, mix some white all-purpose flour in a bowl with a little rice flour or semolina flour (to add a bit of coarseness to the texture). While stirring, add some ice-cold sparkling water until the batter has reached the right consistency, and use to coat the ingredients you want to fry.

Preparation time 10 minutes
Cooking time 20 minutes
Difficulty Easy
Calories 500
Wine Bianco di Capena

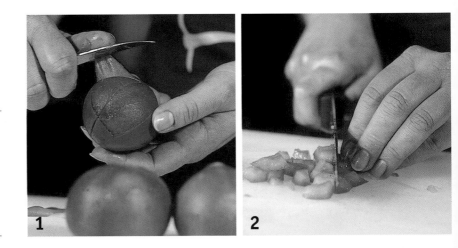

Pumpkin Croquettes
with Cheese

Serves 4

For the croquettes:

1 lb (500 g) green-skinned pumpkin
    flesh
1 white onion
2 Tbsp extra-virgin olive oil
½ lb (200 g) buffalo mozzarella
1 egg
1 cup (150 g) breadcrumbs

To fry:

vegetable oil
salt and pepper

Cut the pumpkin flesh into pieces. Chop the onion and sauté it lightly in a saucepan with the extra-virgin olive oil until transparent.

1. Add the pumpkin (Picture 1) and cook over medium heat, adding a little hot water (or broth) to soften it. Add a dash of salt and pepper and cook until the water on the bottom has condensed.

2. Cool slightly and blend in a food processor. Add the egg and some breadcrumbs until the consistency of the mixture is easy to handle.

3. Dice the mozzarella and make some balls with the pumpkin mixture (either with a scoop or with damp hands). Fill the center of each ball with a small piece of mozzarella (Picture 2) and roll in the breadcrumbs, coating well.

4. Deep fry in very hot vegetable oil (Picture 3) and drain on paper towel; add salt and serve.

Kitchen tip If using a rather soft and watery pumpkin, it is better to cut it into thick slices, grease lightly and bake in the oven so as to make any excessive moisture evaporate. Once cooked, blend the pumpkin in the food processor.

Preparation time 30 minutes
Cooking time 20 minutes
Difficulty Easy
Calories 330
Wine Friuli Isonzo Sauvignon

Cheese Wafers Filled
with Vegetables and Béchamel Sauce

Serves 4

For the wafers:
⅓ lb (110 g) montasio cheese
6 Tbsp grated parmesan
1 small bunch of chives
extra-virgin olive oil

For the vegetable filling:
⅓ lb (140 g) carrots
⅓ lb (140 g) zucchini
¼ lb (120 g) potatoes
1 stalk celery
1 small bunch of chives
3 Tbsp extra-virgin olive oil
salt and pepper

For the béchamel sauce:
1 cup (250 ml) milk
2 pats butter
¼ lb (100 g) brie cheese
3 Tbsp (20 g) all-purpose flour

Preparation time 40 minutes
Cooking time 20 minutes
Difficulty Medium
Calories 463
Wine Rossese di Dolceacqua

Pour all the vegetables, previously cut into matchsticks, into a pan with some warm oil. Add salt and pepper and leave on heat for approx. 10 minutes, so that the vegetables are cooked but still firm to the bite. Drain and put aside.

1. Grease the bottom of a small non-stick pan with some oil. When it is hot, dust the bottom with 2 Tbsp of the cheese mixture made by mixing the grated montasio and parmesan and the chives (Picture 1).

2. Melt the mixture (Picture 2) and, when it has formed a golden crust, remove the pan from heat and spread some of the previously prepared vegetables on the cheese wafers (Picture 3). Roll up the cheese wafers with a knife, so as to form a cylinder (Picture 4), and place on a baking tray.

3. Remove and discard the rind from the brie, dice and boil with some milk in a saucepan. Melt the butter in another saucepan, add the flour and mix. Pour the flour and butter mixture into the milk and cheese one and whisk vigorously with a whip until it comes to the boil.

4. Warm the cheese wafers for 5 minutes in an oven at 350°F (180°C); arrange on plates and add 2 Tbsp of béchamel sauce. Garnish the wafers with a chive stem and serve.

Fried Chicken Nuggets
and Vegetables

Serves 4

For the nuggets:
1 small chicken
1 carrot
1 white onion
2 zucchini
salt

To fry:
⅔ cup (80 g) all-purpose flour
5 Tbsp (50 g) rice flour
2 Tbsp (20 g) semolina flour
sparkling water
extra-virgin olive oil

Remove the skin from the chicken and cut the meat away from the bones, shredding it into bite-sized pieces.

1. Wash the zucchini, trim and cut them in halves (Picture 1) and then into 4 wedges; remove the seeds. Peel the carrot and cut into matchsticks (Picture 2-3). Peel the onion, slice it thinly and cut into rings.

2. Mix the 3 flours in a bowl with a little salt and add the ice-cold water in a thin stream, beating with a fork. Once the batter is fluid and consistent, dip in the vegetables, drain any excess batter and fry.

3. Fry the chicken nuggets after coating them with the batter and drain. Dry on paper towels and salt. Serve immediately.

Kitchen tip You can flavor the batter with some chopped herbs (thyme, marjoram) or with some toasted sesame seeds which will release their aroma after frying and make the texture even crispier.

Preparation time 20 minutes
Cooking time 10 minutes
Difficulty Easy
Calories 329
Wine Prosecco di Conegliano
e Valdobbiadene Brut

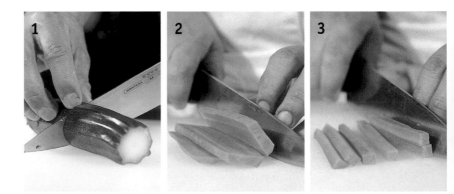

Crisp Beet
and Mushroom Croquettes

Serves 4

For the croquettes:
1 lb (400 g) beet greens
½ lb (250 g) button mushrooms
1 egg
2 Tbsp grated parmesan
¾ cup (100 g) all-purpose flour
1 clove garlic
2 Tbsp extra-virgin olive oil
nutmeg
salt

To fry:
½ cup (50 g) all-purpose flour
¾ cup (100 g) breadcrumbs
1 egg
1 ¾ cups (400 ml) peanut oil

Wash, clean and julienne the beet greens and boil shortly in boiling salted water (Picture 1). Drain and squeeze out excess water, then chop and place in a bowl with 1 egg, the grated Parmesan and ¾ cup (100 g) flour.

1. Clean the mushrooms and cook them whole in olive oil with the garlic clove and a pinch of salt for 10 minutes on a high flame. Drain and chop coarsely.

2. Fold the mushrooms into the beet mixture, add salt and nutmeg and stir until well blended.

3. Form some round, slightly squashed croquettes, coat in the remaining flour, dip in the beaten egg and then cover in breadcrumbs (Picture 1).

4. Fry the croquettes in hot peanut oil, drain on kitchen paper and serve hot.

Some advice To thicken a runny batter add breadcrumbs, flour or some cooked and mashed potatoes: this will set the batter without hardening it too much.

Preparation time 20 minutes
Cooking time 15 minutes
Difficulty Easy
Calories 344
Wine Alto Adige Santa
 Maddalena

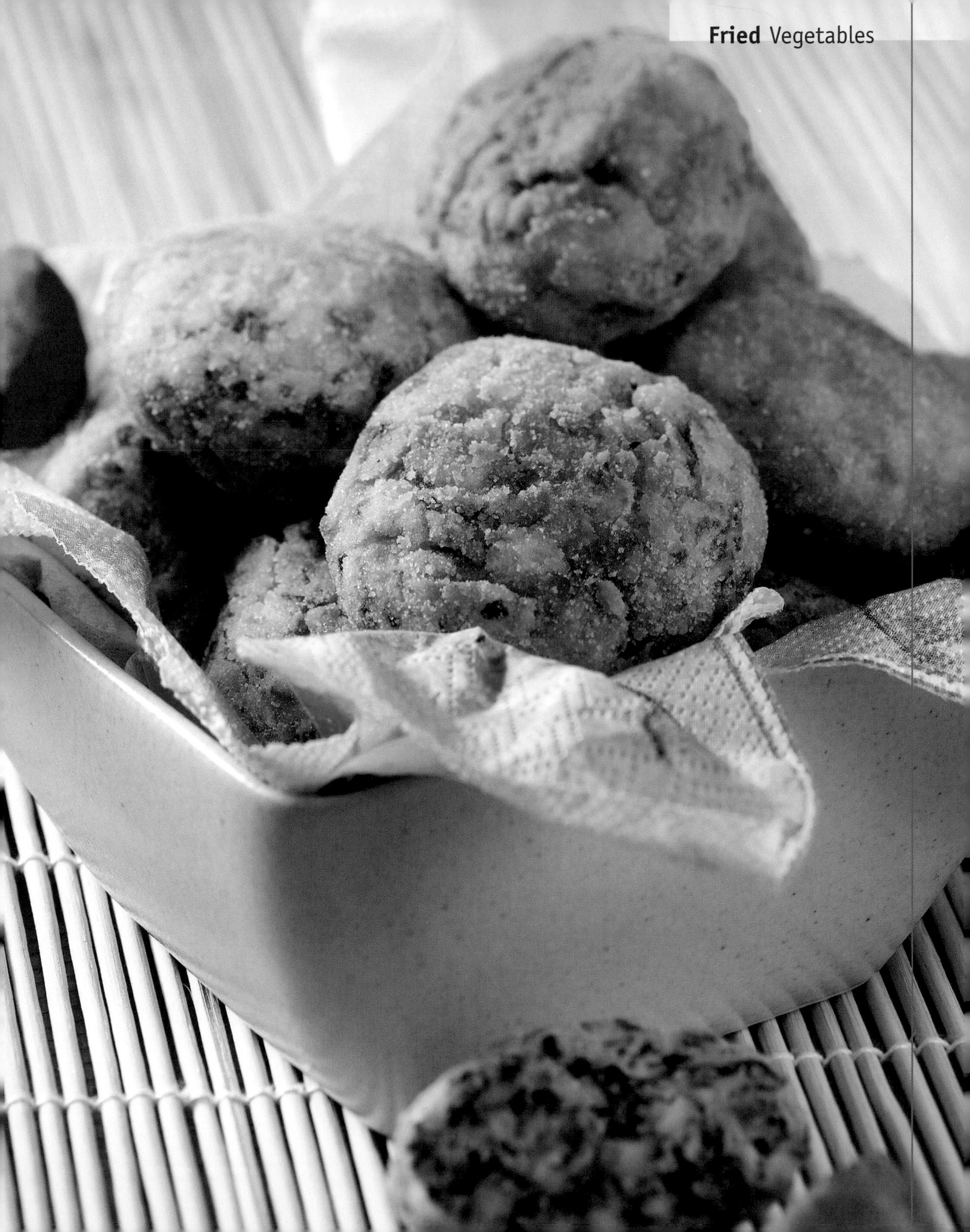

Potato and Savoy Cabbage
Kebabs

Serves 4

For the kebabs:

2 potatoes
¼ Savoy cabbage
1 garlic clove
3 Tbsp extra-virgin olive oil
3 Tbsp cashew nuts
salt and pepper

To fry:

vegetable oil
poppy seeds

Boil the potatoes with their skins on in plenty salted water for approx. 20 minutes. Leave to cool, peel and press them through a potato ricer (Picture 1).

1. Julienne the Savoy cabbage and sauté in a saucepan with the extra-virgin olive oil and the unpeeled garlic clove. Add some water if required and cook until tender but still firm to the bite; add salt and pepper to taste.

2. Add the Savoy cabbage to the potatoes and chopped cashew nuts and wrap around the skewers.

3. Roll the croquettes in the poppy seeds and fry in very hot vegetable oil. Cook until golden and drain on kitchen paper.

An alternative To speed up the preparation, make the croquettes with mashed potatoes. In this case it is better to cook the croquettes in the oven and then place the food on the skewers, alternating the grilled vegetables with the golden croquettes.

Preparation time 20 minutes
Cooking time 20 minutes
Difficulty Easy
Calories 180
Wine Metodo Classico
Franciacorta Brut

1

Vegetable and Chicken
Tempura

Serves 4

For the vegetables and chicken:
¼ lb (200 g) cauliflower
¾ lb (350 g) chicken breast
2 zucchini
1 onion

For the batter:
1 ¼ cup (150 g) all-purpose flour
2 eggs
2 Tbsp chopped herbs
   (parsley, thyme, marjoram, sage)
1 Tbsp extra-virgin olive oil
4 cups (1 l) peanut oil
¾ cup (200 ml) beer
salt

Preparation time 15 minutes
Cooking time 10 minutes
Difficulty Easy
Calories 390
Wine Biferno Rosato

Cut the cauliflower into small florets (Picture 1), blanch in boiling salted water for 3-4 minutes and drain.

1. Peel and slice the onion into rings, rinse well under running water and dry on some kitchen paper. Cut the zucchini into sticks, about ¾ to 1 ¼ in (2-3 cm) long. Prepare the chicken breast by filleting it.

2. Place the flour, egg yolks (Picture 2) and beer (Picture 3) in a bowl; mix with a whisk until the ingredients are well blended. Add the herbs (Picture 4) with a pinch of salt, the extra-virgin olive oil and, last of all, the egg whites, whipped until stiff.

3. Warm the peanut oil in a saucepan with high sides. Dip the pieces of vegetables and chicken in the batter and plunge them into the very hot oil.

4. Fry until the vegetables and the meat are completely golden, then drain with a skimmer and dry on some paper towels. Season with salt and serve immediately.

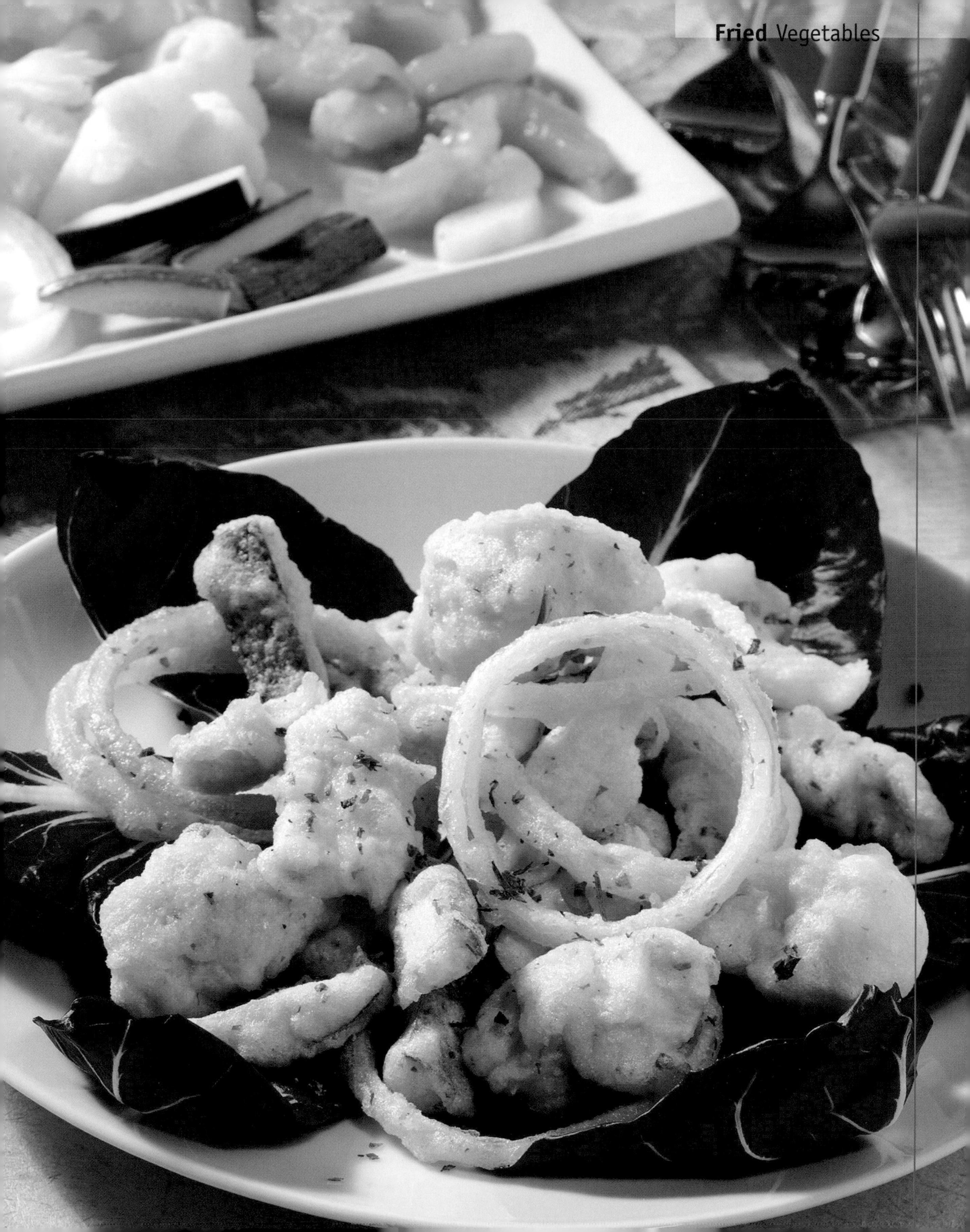

Curry-flavored
Artichoke Croquettes

Serves 4

For the croquettes:
8 artichokes
¾ cup (100 g) all-purpose flour
½ cup (50 g) rice flour
1 tsp curry
sparkling water
salt
vegetable oil

Preparation time 10 minutes
Cooking time 10 minutes
Difficulty Easy
Calories 257
Wine Verduzzo del Friuli

Prepare artichoke hearts by discarding the outer leaves of the artichokes (Picture 1), paring the tops (Picture 2), trimming the base (Picture 3) and removing the inner choke (Picture 4);

1. Mix the 2 flours with the curry and a little salt, add the ice-cold water, beating with a whip until the batter is smooth and rather runny.

2. Plunge the artichokes in the batter and, after draining off the excess coating, fry in very hot oil.

3. Dry the croquettes on some paper towels, season with salt and serve hot.

Kitchen tip The artichoke croquettes can also be baked in the oven. Prepare the artichokes as illustrated above, dip them in a batter made with ¾ cup (100 g) pre-cooked yellow polenta flour and water. Place on non-stick oven paper. Drizzle with oil and bake at 400°F (200°C) for 10-15 minutes.

Baked Vegetables

Asparagus en Croute
with Quail Eggs

Serves 4

For the en croute:

20 large asparagus spears

3 sheets fillo pastry

6 quail eggs

1 tsp poppy seeds

1 pat butter

2 Tbsp extra-virgin olive oil

salt and pepper

Clean the asparagus thoroughly by removing the tough part of the stalk and the outer leaves with a vegetable peeler (Picture 1), cook in boiling salted water until firm to the bite (Picture 2) and leave to cool in water and ice.

1. Boil the quail eggs for 2 minutes in hot water. Roll out the sheets of fillo pastry and cut out 20 strips, about 2 in (5 cm) long. Wrap the pastry strips around the asparagus and brush with melted butter. Dust with poppy seeds and bake at 400°F (200°C) for 20 minutes.

2. Crumble the eggs by hand and sprinkle over the crispy asparagus. Dress with a little oil, salt and pepper.

Interesting to know Quail eggs can be employed in the same way as chicken eggs: soft-boiled, hard-boiled, sunny-side up, in cakes and desserts or in unusual tagliatelle.

Preparation time 15 minutes
Cooking time 20 minutes
Difficulty Easy
Calories 189
Wine Soave

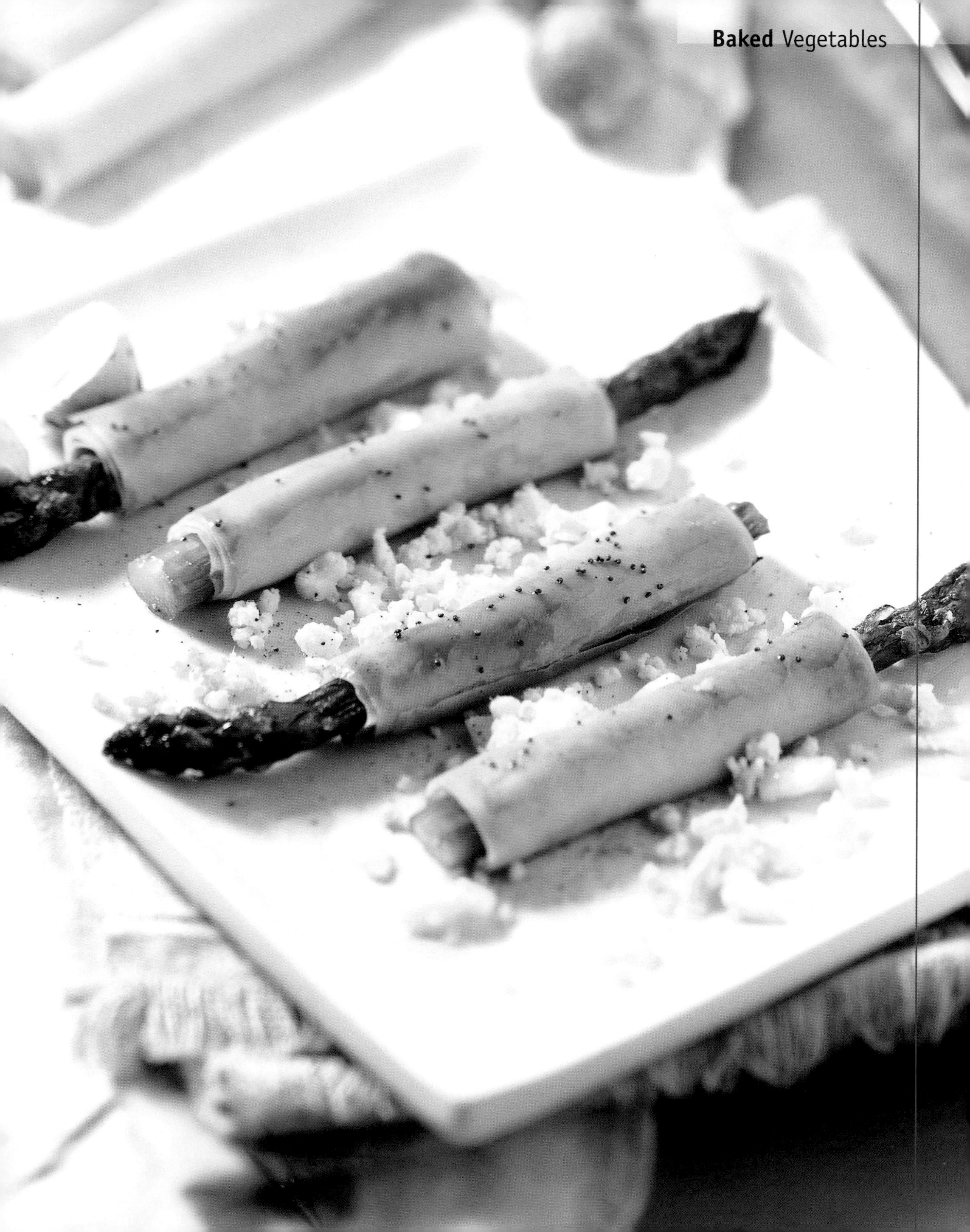

Vegetarian
Loaf

Serves 4

For the loaf:
6-7 zucchini
2 carrots
1 cup (200 g) frozen peas
½ cup milk
10 slices of white sandwich bread
2 eggs
1 handful breadcrumbs
2 cups (200 g) grated parmesan
salt and pepper

Preparation time 15 minutes
Cooking time 15 minutes
Difficulty Easy
Calories 330
Wine Cinque Terre Bianco

Slice the zucchini into thick rounds leaving 1 whole. Place in a container in the microwave with 2 tablespoons of water; close and cook at full power for 8 minutes. In alternative, cook the zucchini in a steam basket on the stovetop.

1. Peel the carrots, dice and cook with the peas for 7 minutes.

2. Remove the crust from the bread and soak in milk. In a separate bowl, whisk the eggs with a little salt and pepper.

3. Place all the vegetables in a bowl and leave to cool. Gently squeeze out the excess milk from the bread (Picture 1) and add it with the breadcrumbs and beaten eggs to the vegetables (Pictures 2-3). Dust with parmesan, season to taste and unmold the mixture onto a sheet of non-stick oven paper; close the paper in the shape of a loaf.

4. Wash and trim the remaining zucchini, slice into thin rounds and arrange on top of the loaf (Picture 4). Close the paper again and bake in oven at 375°F (190°C) for 35-40 minutes. Leave the loaf to cool and serve sliced.

Stewed Belgian Endive
au Gratin

Serves 4

For the au gratin:
4 heads Belgian endive
1 Tbsp raisins
3 Tbsp extra-virgin olive oil
3 Tbsp breadcrumbs
2 garlic cloves
1 Tbsp pine nuts
½ cup (100 ml) vegetable broth
2 Tbsp vinegar
thyme
salt

Soak the raisins in hot broth. Crush the unpeeled garlic and sauté in oil until golden.

1. Cut the endive vertically into 4 pieces (Picture 1). In a separate pan, lightly toast the pine nuts (Picture 2), remove from heat and put aside.

2. Add the raisins to the sautéed garlic, together with the pine nuts and the endive. Cook for 5-6 minutes, season with salt and add vinegar.

3. When the vinegar has evaporated, add the hot broth and cook covered for a few minutes. Once cooked, dust with breadcrumbs and place under a broiler. Serve the endive dusted with thyme.

Kitchen tip A tasty variation can be made using red radicchio. To obtain a completely different flavor, use some small onions, cooking them slightly longer than the endive.

Preparation time 10 minutes
Cooking time 15 minutes
Difficulty Easy
Calories 195
Wine Val Venosta Riesling

1

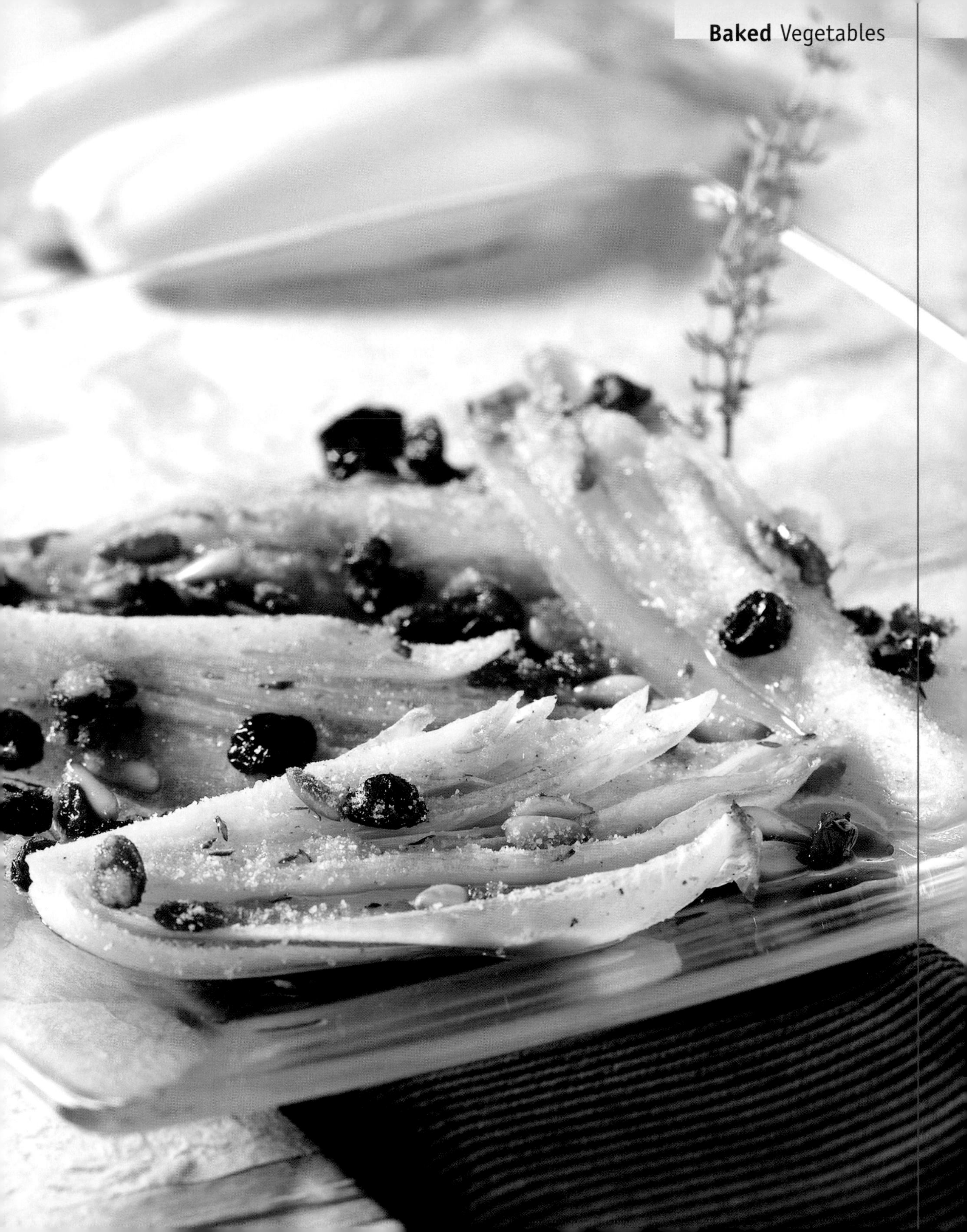

Potato
and Mushroom Bake

Serves 4-6

For the pastry shell:
2 ¼ lbs (1 kg) potatoes
1 ⅔ cup (400 ml) milk
½ lb (180 g) stringy cheese (scamorza, mozzarella, etc.)
½ stick (50 g) butter
5 Tbsp grated parmesan cheese
1 handful dried mushrooms
1 cup beer
1 garlic clove
3 Tbsp extra-virgin olive oil
salt

Place the mushrooms in the beer and leave to soak for about 30 minutes.

1. In the meantime, peel and clean the potatoes, cut into small pieces and cook the in the milk. Pass through a potato ricer and mix with butter, parmesan (Picture 1) and salt. Put the mash aside and leave to cool.

2. Slice the garlic and sauté in a pan with a little oil. Add the squeezed mushrooms and simmer until the liquid has evaporated.

3. Stir the mash, mushrooms and diced cheese until well blended and place in a greased oven dish (Picture 2). Bake au gratin at 350°F (180°C) for 20 minutes in a ventilated oven until a crust forms; remove from heat and serve hot.

Kitchen tip In autumn the dried mushrooms can be replaced with fresh ones. Use a combination of oyster mushrooms, honey mushrooms and porcini mushrooms: clean, thinly slice and sauté them with garlic, extra-virgin olive oil and parsley. Once cooked, add the mushrooms to the mashed potatoes.

Preparation time 45 minutes
Cooking time 40 minutes
Difficulty Easy
Calories 415
Wine Dolcetto di Ovada

1   2

Eggplant
Roulades

Serves 4

For the roulades:

2 medium eggplant
²⁄₃ lb (300g) ground meat
1 egg
2 Tbsp grated parmesan cheese
1 stale roll
1 small bunch of parsley
4 Tbsp extra-virgin olive oil
¾ cup (200 g) tomato purée
¼ lb (100 g) provola cheese
salt

To fry:

2 ⅓ cups (600 ml) vegetable oil

Preparation time 20 minutes
Cooking time 40 minutes
Difficulty Easy
Calories 310
Wine Bianco d'Alcamo

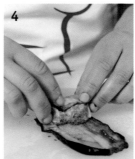

Slice the eggplant, place on a plate and sprinkle with salt (Picture 1). Leave to rest for approx. 20 minutes.

1. Mix the minced meat in a bowl with the egg, chopped parsley and parmesan (Picture 2). Soak the bread in some salted water and add to the meat. Form some balls and put aside (Picture 3).

2. Fry the eggplant in a pan and dry on some paper towels. Roll the slices of eggplant around every meat ball to form roulades (Picture 4).

3. Grease an oven dish, pour some tomato purée and arrange the roulades. Cover with the remaining tomato purée and the sliced provola, dust with parmesan and bake at 350°F (180°C) for approx. 30 minutes.

4. Serve the eggplant roulades piping hot.

Kitchen tip Prepare a vegetarian version of this dish in the following way: soak the stale bread in water, drain and add some parmesan and some chopped green olives and capers. Add 1 Tbsp of pesto to taste, fill the eggplants with this mixture and proceed according to recipe directions.

Asparagus
and Ham Omelet

Serves 4

For the omelet:

6 eggs

8 Tbsp grated parmesan cheese

4 slices (120 g) cooked ham

½ tsp nutmeg

2 small slices (50 g) emmental
cheese

1 small bunch of chives

⅔ lb (300 g) asparagus

1 pat butter

salt and pepper

Preparation time 20 minutes
Cooking time 25 minutes
Difficulty Easy
Calories 400
Wine Müller Thurgau

Clean the asparagus and bring some lightly salted water to a boil. Boil the asparagus for approx. 10 minutes, drain and put aside.

1. Cut the ham and the emmental into small pieces. Break the eggs in a bowl and add the nutmeg, salt, pepper, half of the grated parmesan and the diced emmental and ham (Pictures 1-2).

2. Add the chopped chives and stir until well blended.

3. Melt a pat of butter in a pan, pour in part of the egg mixture and cook the omelet until the bottom part is firm. Place a couple of asparagus on the omelet (Picture 3) and dust with grated parmesan.

4. Lift one side of the omelet with a spatula and fold it over, forming a closed parcel (Picture 4): the inner part must be very moist. Cook the closed omelet for a few seconds and remove from pan. Keep warm and prepare the other omelets in the same way. Serve hot.

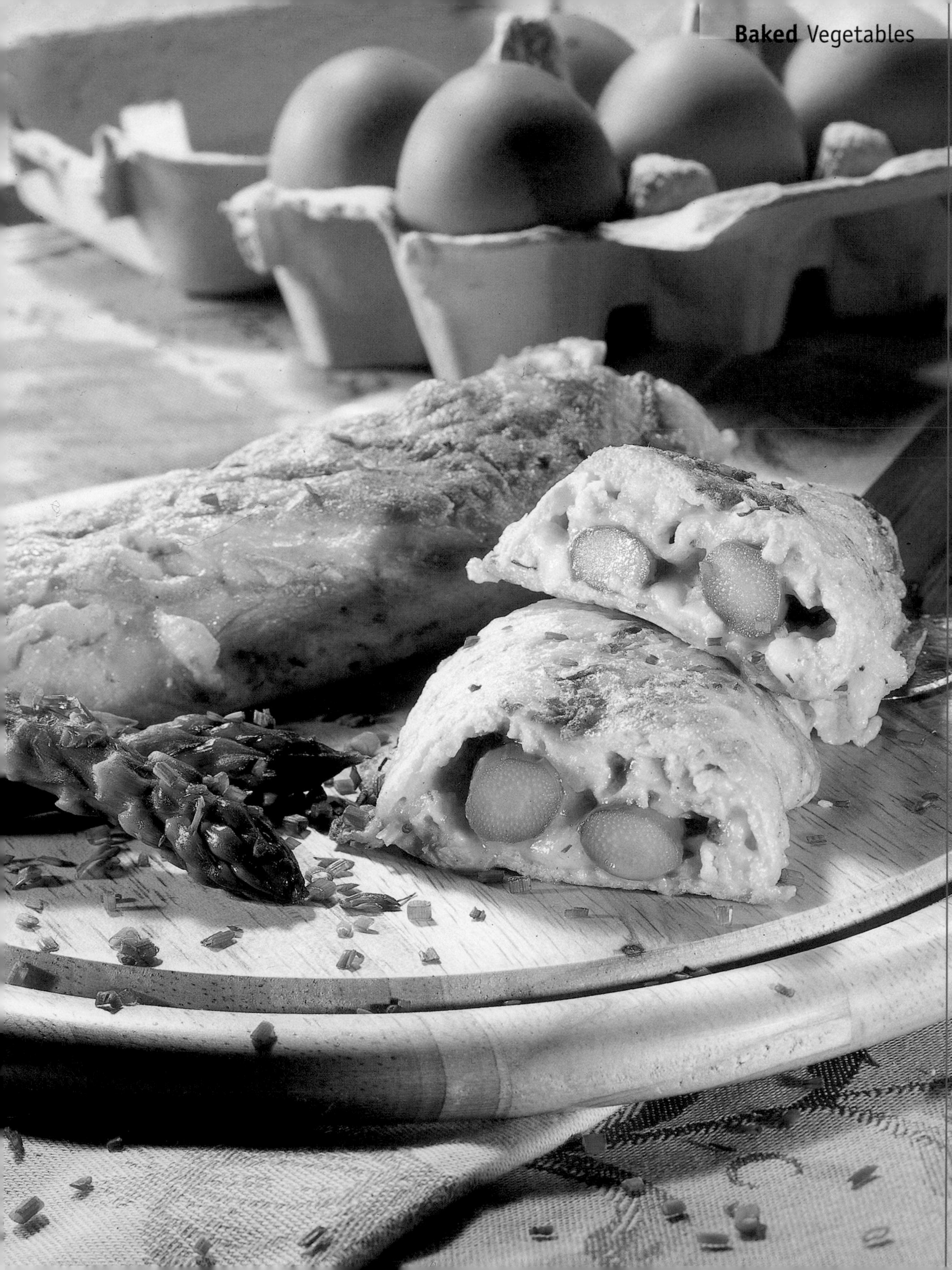

Bean Timbales
with Parmesan

Serves 4

For the timbales:
½ cup (120 g) white beans
1 egg
1 shallot
2 bay leaves
chives
salt

For the pancakes:
4 carrots
4 long potatoes
all-purpose flour
salt

For the sauce:
2 leeks
2 bay leaves
2 Tbsp extra-virgin olive oil
vegetable broth

In addition:
extra-virgin olive oil
grated parmesan

Preparation time 25 minutes
Cooking time 2 hours
Difficulty Medium
Calories 255
Wine Vernaccia di S. Gimignano

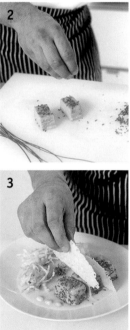

Soak the beans overnight. Once the beans have softened, place them in water with 2 bay leaves and cook until tender, then drain and set aside.

1. Stew the shallot in a little oil and add to the beans (keep a few whole ones aside for garnishing), together with some vegetable broth and 1 egg. Blend, sieve (Picture 1) and add salt.

2. Fill 4 muffin cups and cook for 25–30 minutes at 325°F (160°C). Remove from oven and cut each timbale into 3 parts. Dust with chives (Picture 2) and keep warm.

3. Thinly shred the carrots and potatoes with a mandolin slicer. Form some small balls with the aid of a little water and flour. Fry in oil at 350°F (170°C), add salt and keep warm.

4. Stew the leeks with the bay leaves in two Tbsp of oil and some vegetable broth. Sieve until smooth and creamy.

5. Cover most of the plate with the cream, place the timbale on one side and insert the grated parmesan (Picture 3) in-between the three parts. Place the pancakes on the other side (Picture 4) and decorate with the remaining whole beans.

Savoy Cabbage Leaves Stuffed
with Rice, Meat and Vegetables

Serves 6-8

For the stuffed cabbage leaves:
½ lb (200 g) ground meat
1 cup (100 g) rice for soup
½ cup (100 g) tomato paste
5 Tbsp sunflower oil
2 ¼ lbs (1 kg) Savoy cabbage
2 onions
1 medium carrot
1 bell pepper
1 egg
salt and pepper

Clean the vegetables: peel the carrot, slice the bell pepper in half, remove the seeds and white part and clean the onion. Dice the vegetables (Picture 1) and sauté in the sunflower oil for 5 minutes. Add the rice (Picture 2), stir, remove from heat and leave to cool.

1. Add the rice mixture to the minced meat (Picture 3) with the tomato paste, egg, salt and pepper and stir until well blended.

2. Blanch the cabbage leaves one by one in boiling water. Leave to cool and form some small parcels by wrapping a Tbsp of the meat mixture in every cabbage leaf (Picture 4).

3. Place in a saucepan with some salted water and boil on a low flame for 40 minutes. Serve hot.

Interesting to know This is a typical Romanian dish. An alternative, closer to the original recipe, replaces the Savoy cabbage leaves with grape leaves.

Preparation time 25 minutes
Cooking time 1 hour and
          45 minutes
Difficulty Easy
Calories 287
Wine Verdicchio di Matelica

Ricotta Cheese and Potato Timbales
with Radicchio Sauce

Serves 4-6

For the timbales:
½ lb (200 g) potatoes
1 ¼ cups (300 g) ricotta cheese
2 eggs
2 egg whites
2 bunches radicchio
2 Tbsp extra-virgin olive oil
1 Tbsp all-purpose flour
1 ¼ cups (300 ml) vegetable broth
breadcrumbs
nutmeg
salt and pepper

Preparation time 15 minutes
Cooking time 1 hour and
　　　　　　　　15 minutes
Difficulty Easy
Calories 150
Wine Fiano di Avellino

Boil the potatoes in plenty of boiling salted water, peel and pass through a food mill together with the ricotta (Picture 1), then place in a bowl.

1. Add the whole eggs and the egg whites, whipped until stiff (Picture 2). Season with salt and pepper and some nutmeg.

2. Grease 6 aluminum ramekins (Picture 3) and dust with breadcrumbs; add the potato, ricotta and egg mixture and bake at 350°F (180°C) for 20 minutes.

3. Warm some oil in a saucepan and simmer the radicchio cut into strips for 2-3 minutes. Sprinkle with 1 Tbsp of flour, mix, add the broth (Picture 4), season with salt and pepper and cook for 10 minutes. Blend the sauce with an immersion blender and adjust to taste.

4. Serve the ricotta and potato timbales piping hot with the radicchio sauce and garnish with whole or shredded radicchio leaves.

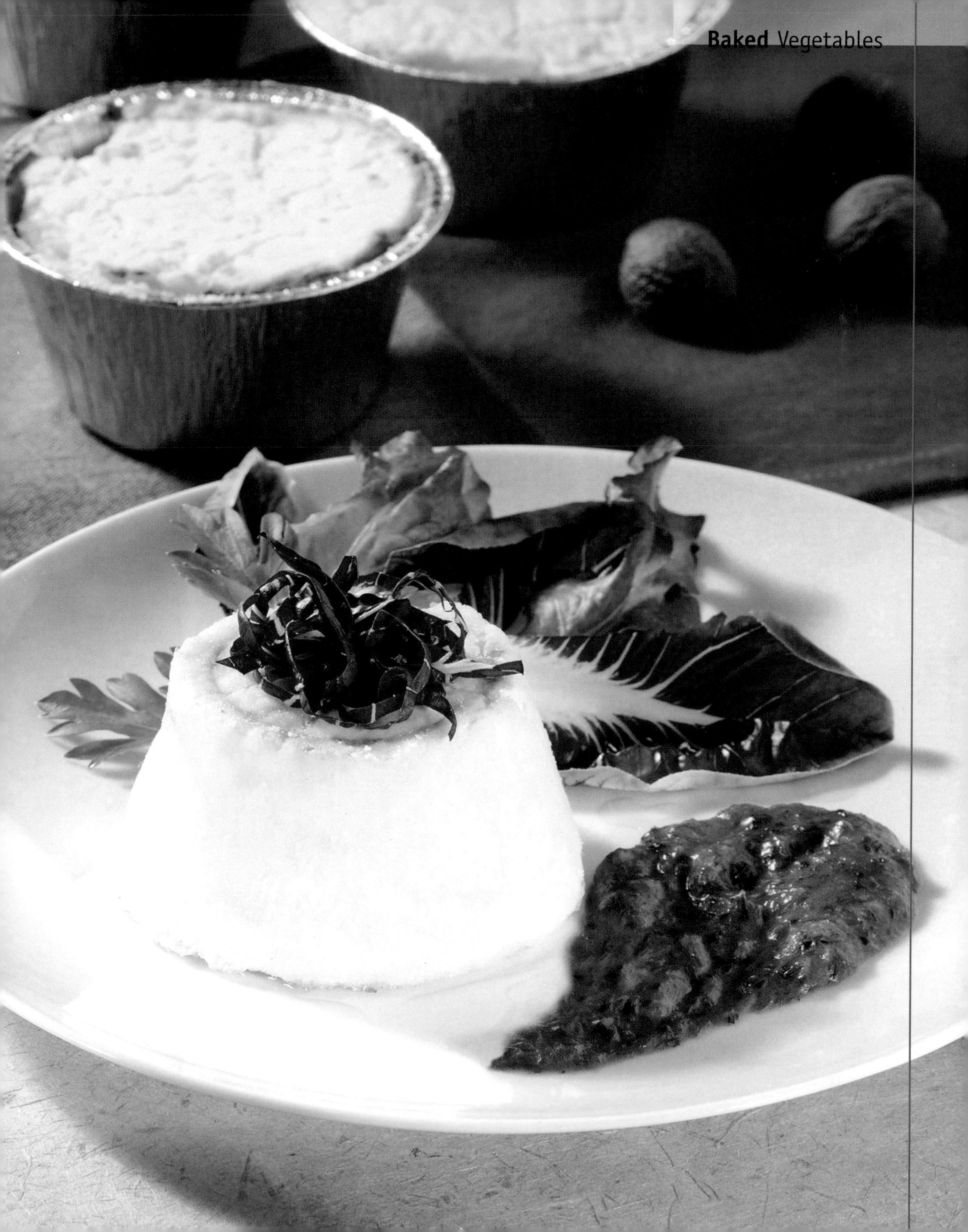

Parmesan Baskets
with Vegetables and Parmesan Sauce

Serves 4

For the baskets:
2 cups (200 g) grated parmesan

For the parmesan sauce:
1 egg
2 yolks
4 Tbsp grated parmesan cheese
5 Tbsp (50 ml) fresh cream
5 Tbsp (50 ml) milk
2 pats butter
2 Tbsp extra-virgin olive oil
salt and pepper

For the vegetables:
2 artichokes
1 small bunch asparagus
1 shallot
1 ½ cups (200 g) snow peas
¼ lb (200 g) string beans
¾ cup (100 g) peas, shelled
¾ cup (100 g) fresh fava beans,
  shelled

Preparation time 35 minutes
Cooking time 15 minutes
Difficulty Medium
Calories 481
Wine Trebbiano di Romagna

Trim, wash and cook all the vegetables separately in boiling salted water. Drain when firm to the bite and cool in water and ice.

1. Warm a pan and cover the bottom with a thin layer of grated parmesan. Once the cheese starts to melt and forms a slight crust, turn it over (Picture 1), heat for a few seconds and then arrange into a small upturned cup; leave to cool after pressing the cheese into a basket shape.

2. Pour all the sauce ingredients into a saucepan and cook in a double boiler over medium heat, whisking with a whip (Picture 2) until light and fluffy.

3. Thoroughly clean the asparagus and the string beans and cut in halves. Warm 2 Tbsp of oil with the finely chopped shallot in a non-stick pan; add the asparagus and the string beans and sauté over high heat for a few minutes (Picture 3). Add salt and pepper.

4. When the parmesan baskets have cooled and solidified, overturn them delicately and fill with the warm vegetables (Picture 4). Serve the baskets, slightly warm, on some parmesan sauce in individual plates.

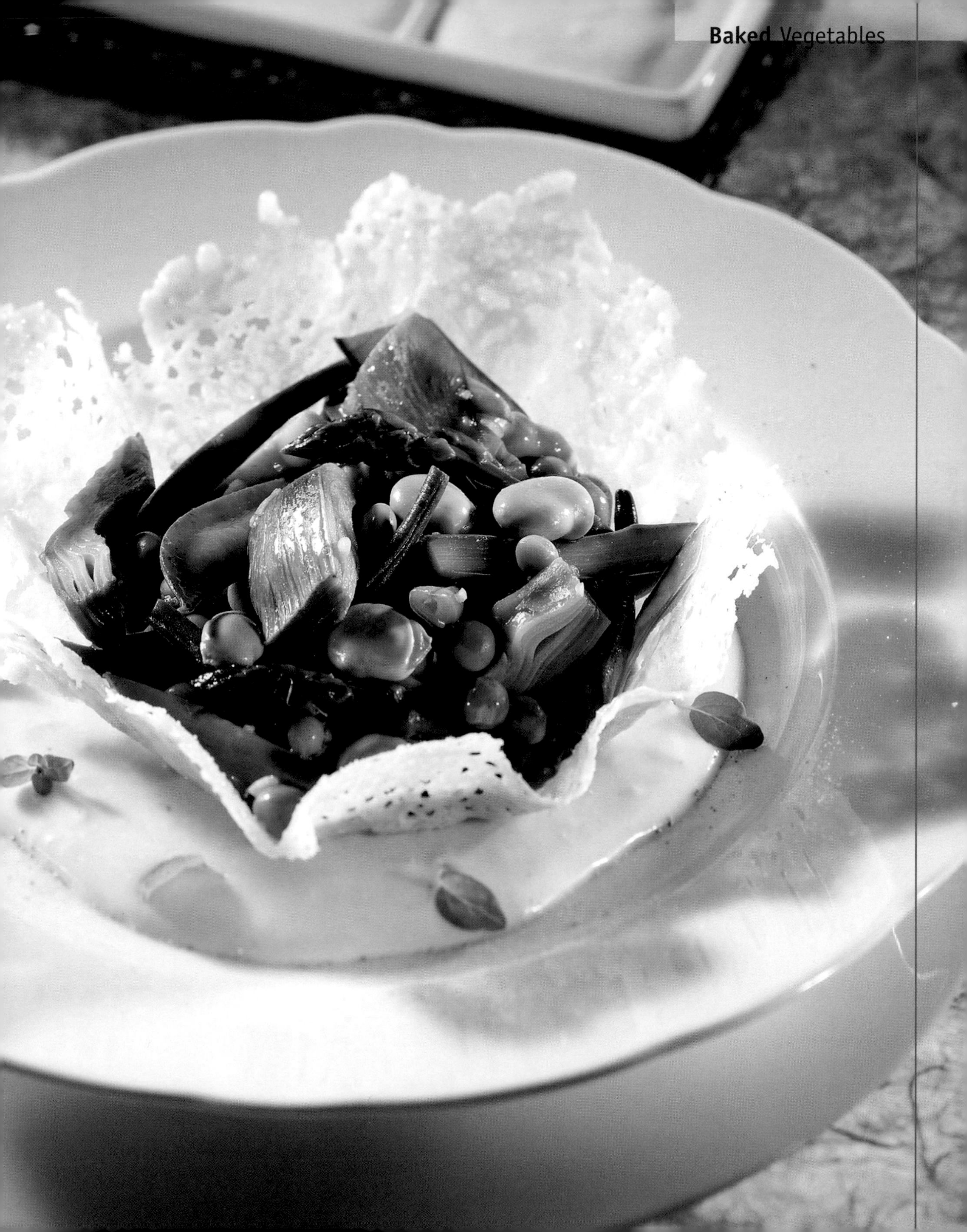

Vegetable Terrine
in a Potato Crust

Serves 4

For the terrine:

⅔ lb (300 g) string beans

⅔ lb (300 g) peas

½ lb (200 g) cauliflower

3 small zucchini

3 small carrots

1 onion

5-6 potatoes

⅕ lb (100 g) scamorza cheese

4 thick slices (100 g) smoked
  pancetta

4 Tbsp extra-virgin olive oil

2 cups (½ l) milk

1 stick (110 g) butter

5 Tbsp all-purpose flour

3 Tbsp grated parmesan cheese

1 egg

salt

Preparation time 40 minutes
Cooking time 30 minutes
Difficulty Easy
Calories 550
Wine Bianco di Scandiano

Melt 3 pats of butter (50 g) in a pan, add the flour and mix well. Slowly add milk in a thin stream to obtain a firm béchamel sauce. Season with salt and leave to cool.

1. Clean the vegetables, boil them all (apart from the potatoes and the onion) and, once they have cooled, cut into pieces. Slice the onion finely and fry slowly in oil; add the diced pancetta (Picture 1) and the boiled vegetables (Picture 2). Leave to simmer for a few minutes.

2. Whisk the egg with the parmesan and pour it into the béchamel sauce. Add the vegetables (Picture 3) and the diced scamorza.

3. Peel the potatoes and cut into thin slices. Grease an oven dish with part of the remaining butter (about 1 ½ pat of butter or 30 g) and line the bottom and the edges with a layer of potatoes.

4. Fill with the vegetable mixture (Picture 4) and cover with another layer of potatoes. Dust with a pinch of salt, add some small pats of butter and bake at 350°F (180°C) for 25 minutes until the potatoes are golden. Serve the terrine after leaving it to cool for a few minutes.

Stuffed Savoy
Cabbage Roll

Serves 4-6

For the roll:

1 small Savoy cabbage
4 large potatoes
3 pats butter
8 Tbsp grated parmesan cheese
1 egg
½ lb (250 g) frozen spinach
1 carrot
nutmeg
salt

For the sauce:

½ lemon
4 Tbsp extra-virgin olive oil
salt

Preparation time 30 minutes
Cooking time 40 minutes
Difficulty Easy
Calories 310
Wine Verdicchio di Matelica

Remove the tougher leaves from the cabbage, wash and blanch the remaining leaves in boiling water. Drain and arrange them in layers, forming a rectangle.

1. Boil the potatoes, press them through a potato ricer and put in a saucepan with 1 ½ pat (30 g) of butter. Season with salt and reduce the purée over low heat. Add some parmesan, a pinch of nutmeg and an egg and stir until well blended (Picture 1).

2. Blanch the spinach for a few minutes, chop, season with salt and dry out over gentle heat with the remaining butter. Boil the carrot in a little water and put aside.

3. Spread the potato purée over the cabbage leaves (Picture 2), place the spinach in the center (Picture 3) and finish off with the whole carrot. Wrap the cabbage leaves around the filling in the shape of a roll, enclose in a sheet of kitchen foil (Picture 4) and place in the refrigerator for 2 hours.

4. Remove the roll from the refrigerator, slice and dress with oil, lemon juice and salt.

Stuffed Zucchini
with Ham

Serves 4

For the zucchini:

5 zucchini
8 slices (200 g) cooked ham
3 slices (100 g) mortadella
¾ cup (100 g) breadcrumbs
½ lb (200 g) mozzarella
1 ¼ cups (300 g) crushed tomatoes
2 eggs
5 Tbsp grated parmesan cheese
1 small bunch parsley
1 garlic clove
1 pat butter
salt and pepper
extra-virgin olive oil

Preparation time 15 minutes
Cooking time 35 minutes
Difficulty Easy
Calories 651
Wine Ortrugo

Thoroughly wash the zucchini and cut in halves. Remove the flesh, cut into pieces, and sauté in a pan with a little oil and put aside.

1. Chop the ham and the mortadella, slice the mozzarella (Picture 1) and then cut it into pieces.

2. Put the mortadella, ham, eggs, parsley, grated garlic, breadcrumbs, half of the grated parmesan and some of the mozzarella in a bowl and stir (Picture 2). Work the mixture by hand, adding the zucchini flesh and mixing well.

3. Stuff the hollowed zucchini with the filling (Picture 3) and place on a greased oven dish. Pour the crushed tomatoes over the top (Picture 4) and bake at 350°F (180°C) for approx. 25 minutes.

4. Add the remaining pieces of mozzarella and dust with some parmesan. Place in oven for another 5 minutes until the cheese melts. Remove from oven and leave to cool before serving.

Eggplant Rollups
with Raisins and Pine Nuts

Serves 4

For the rollups:
⅔ lb (300 g) eggplant
⅓ lb (150 g) zucchini
¼ lb (80 g) red bell pepper
¼ lb (80 g) yellow bell pepper
¼ lb (80 g) green bell pepper
6 Tbsp (50 g) raisins
5 Tbsp (40 g) pine nuts
1 small bunch of chives
4 Tbsp extra-virgin olive oil
1 garlic clove
salt and pepper

Preparation time 30 minutes
Cooking time 15 minutes
Difficulty Easy
Calories 210
Wine Inzolia

1

2

3

Put the raisins in boiling water and leave to soak. In the meantime, clean and cut the bell peppers in halves, remove the stem, seeds and the white parts inside.

1. Wash the zucchini, trim and cut in halves lengthwise. Cut the bell peppers and the zucchini into thin matchsticks (Pictures 1-2): put the vegetables in a bowl.

2. Wash, peel and cut the eggplant into slices about 0.1 in (3-4 mm) thick, arrange on a tray and dress with a little salt and oil.

3. Warm up a cast iron griddle: when hot, place the eggplant slices on it, grilling them on both sides (Picture 3); once cooked, put on a tray.

4. Sauté a clove of garlic in a pan with some oil, add the bell peppers and the sliced zucchini and cook for 3-4 minutes over a high flame. Add salt and pepper, together with the pine nuts and the softened raisins (Picture 4). Stir the mixture until well blended and cook for another 4 minutes, dusting with a small bunch of finely chopped chives. Remove from heat and put aside.

5. Lay the eggplant slices on a working surface and stuff with a Tbsp of cooked vegetables. Wrap the slices up, forming roulades, and arrange on the plates with the remaining vegetables. Dust the roulades with chopped chives and serve immediately.

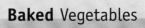

Crustless Potato Quiches
with Curry Sauce

Serves 4

For the quiches:

5 potatoes

⅓ cup (100 ml) fresh cream

4 Tbsp grated parmesan cheese

2 thick slices (40 g) bacon

1 pat butter

2 eggs

salt and pepper

For the sauce:

⅔ cup (150 ml) fresh cream

2 Tbsp all-purpose flour

½ onion

2 Tbsp curry powder

2 Tbsp extra-virgin olive oil

salt

For garnishing:

1 small bunch of parsley

Boil 3 potatoes in a saucepan of lightly salted boiling water and press through a potato ricer. Put the mashed potatoes in a bowl and leave to cool, add the eggs, grated parmesan, diced bacon (Picture 1) and cream; season with salt and pepper and stir until well blended.

1. Take the remaining 2 potatoes, trim them into cylinders, slice thinly with a vegetable slicer and blanch in boiling water for 1 minute. Drain and put aside.

2. Grease 4 muffin cups, line with the potatoes sliced into rounds (Picture 2), fill with the potato and bacon mixture and bake in a hot oven at 350°F (180°C) for 30 minutes.

3. Toast the onion in a saucepan with the oil hot. Add the curry, a pinch of salt, the flour and cream. Bring to the boil and leave to thicken slightly. Purée the mixture until smooth and creamy.

4. Remove the quiches, overturn them in the plates and serve with the curry sauce. Garnish with some parsley and serve immediately.

Preparation time 30 minutes
Cooking time 1 hour and 20 minutes
Difficulty Medium
Calories 459
Wine Greco di Tufo

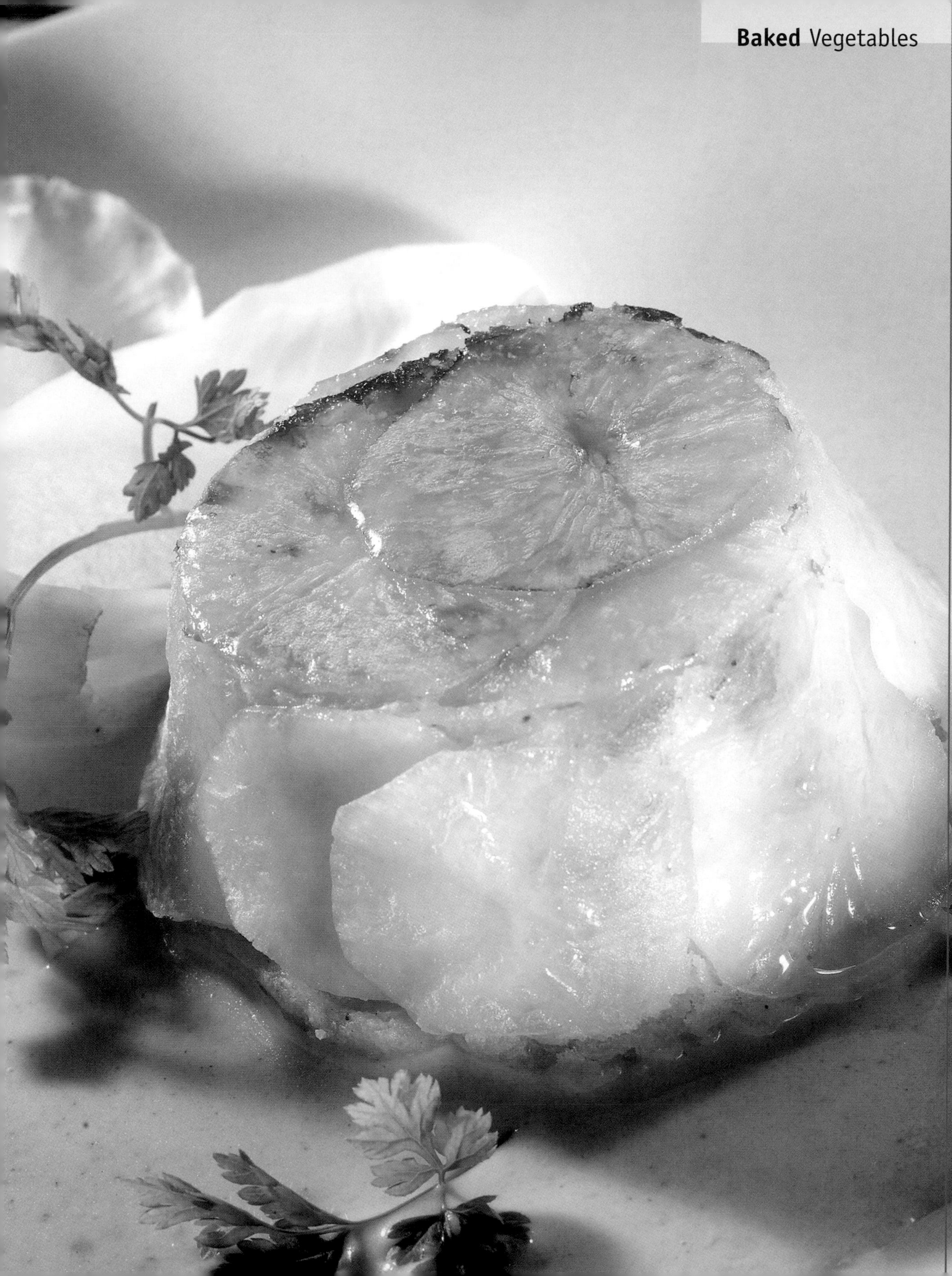

Jerusalem Artichoke Timbales
with Bacon in Cheese Sauce

Serves 6

For the timbales:
1 ¼ cups (300 ml) milk
⅓ cup (50 g) all-purpose flour
2 pats butter
2 Tbsp extra-virgin olive oil
3 eggs
⅔ lb (300 g) jerusalem artichoke
7 Tbsp grated parmesan cheese
4 thick slices (80 g) bacon
salt and pepper

For the cheese sauce:
1 cup (250 ml) cream
¼ lb (130 g) brie
salt and pepper

For the ramekins:
2 pats butter

Preparation time 20 minutes
Cooking time 1 hour
Difficulty Easy
Calories 468
Wine Trentino Nosiola

1

2

3

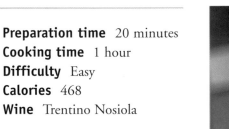

4

Peel the jerusalem artichoke (Picture 1) and boil in salted water for about 15 minutes. Drain, dice and put aside.

1. Dice the bacon and sauté in a pan with some oil. Remove from heat and add to the jerusalem artichoke (Picture 2); stir and put aside.

2. Melt the butter in a saucepan without making it fry. Quickly add the flour and stir until the mixture is smooth and well blended. Add the milk in a thin stream and cook over moderate heat, season with salt and pepper and stir until the mixture thickens.

3. Pour this béchamel sauce in a bowl: add the eggs, bacon and jerusalem artichoke mixture (Picture 3) and the grated parmesan. Mix until all the ingredients are well blended.

4. Grease some aluminum ramekins and fill up to 3/4 with the mixture (Picture 4). Arrange in oven dish half filled with water, place in oven and cook for 30 minutes at 325°F (170°C).

5. Melt the brie in a small saucepan with the cream, season to taste and cook over moderate heat until the sauce is thick and creamy. Remove the timbales from the oven, overturn them onto the plates and serve with the cheese sauce.

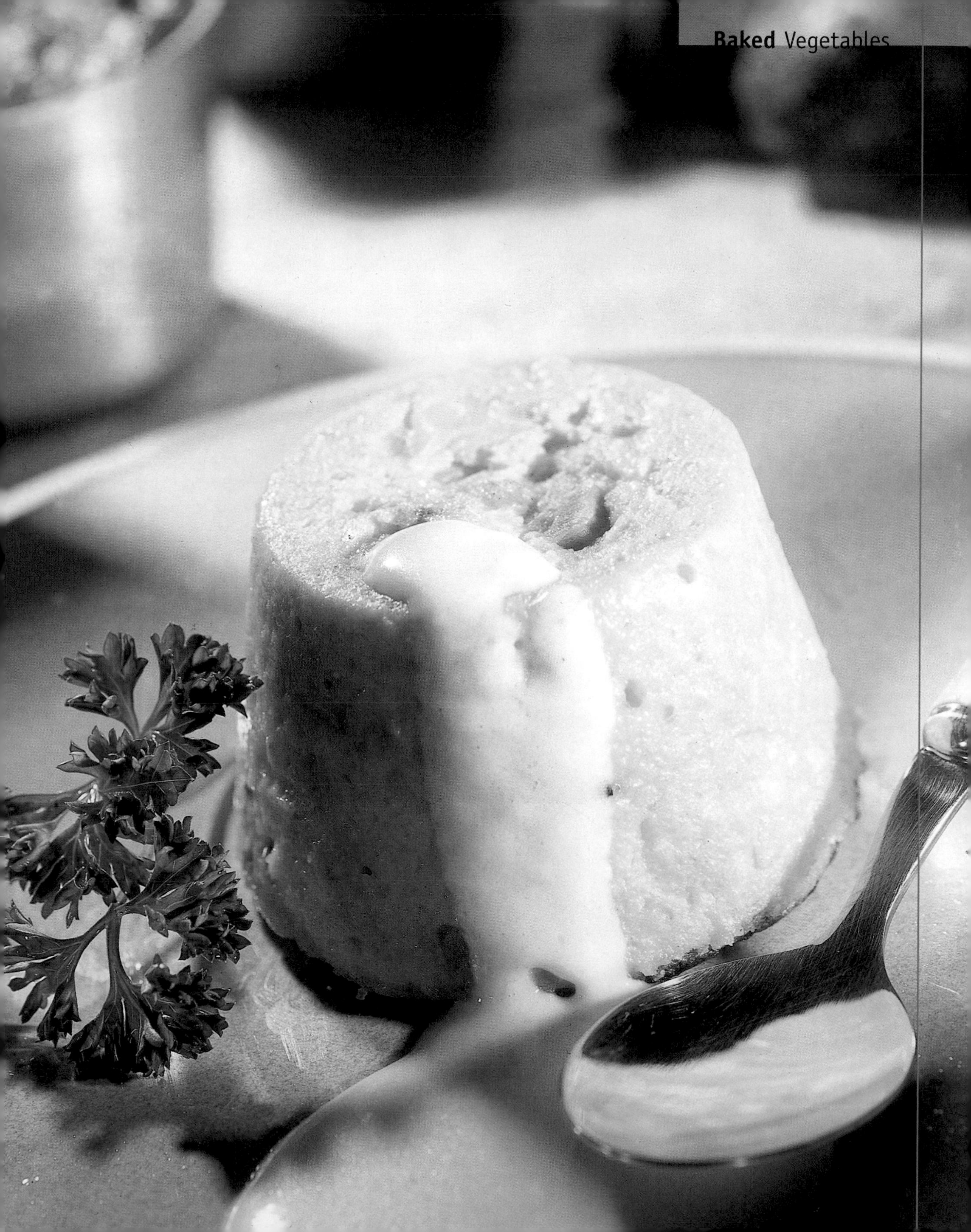

Artichokes
in Cheese Sauce

Serves 4

For the artichokes:
8 artichokes (800 g)

For the cheese sauce:
5-6 thyme sprigs
2 Tbsp extra-virgin olive oil
5 Tbsp (50 ml) fresh cream
¼ lb (100 g) brie
1 egg yolk
5 Tbsp grated parmesan cheese
2 Tbsp granulated almonds

For garnishing:
2 Tbsp grated parmesan cheese

Bring a saucepan of water to the boil and salt lightly. Remove the stem from the artichokes with a sharp knife and discard the tough outer leaves. Open the inner leaves slightly and, with a scoop, clean the artichoke heart thoroughly (Picture 1), so as to obtain a small container for the brie fondue.

1. Finely chop the thyme leaves with a crescent cutter. Clean the brie by removing the rind, break it into pieces and put in a pan.

2. Add the cream and melt the cheese, stirring constantly over a low to moderate flame, ensuring a velvety-smooth sauce. Remove from heat and pour the egg yolk into the mixture: continue to stir with the Tbsp and add the grated parmesan, the chopped thyme and the granulated almonds.

3. Set the oven at 325°F (170°C). Grease the bottom of an oven dish with some oil. Fill the emptied artichokes with 1 or 2 spoons of the brie sauce (Picture 2).

4. Dust the stuffed artichokes with some grated parmesan and place in oven: cook au gratin for approx. 10 minutes. Remove from oven and serve immediately.

Preparation time 25 minutes
Cooking time 20 minutes
Difficulty Medium
Calories 286
Wine Trebbiano di Romagna

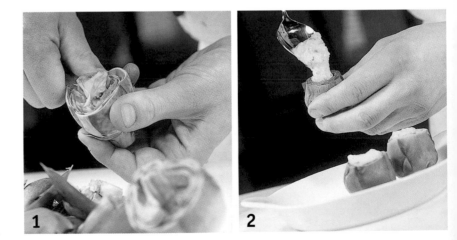

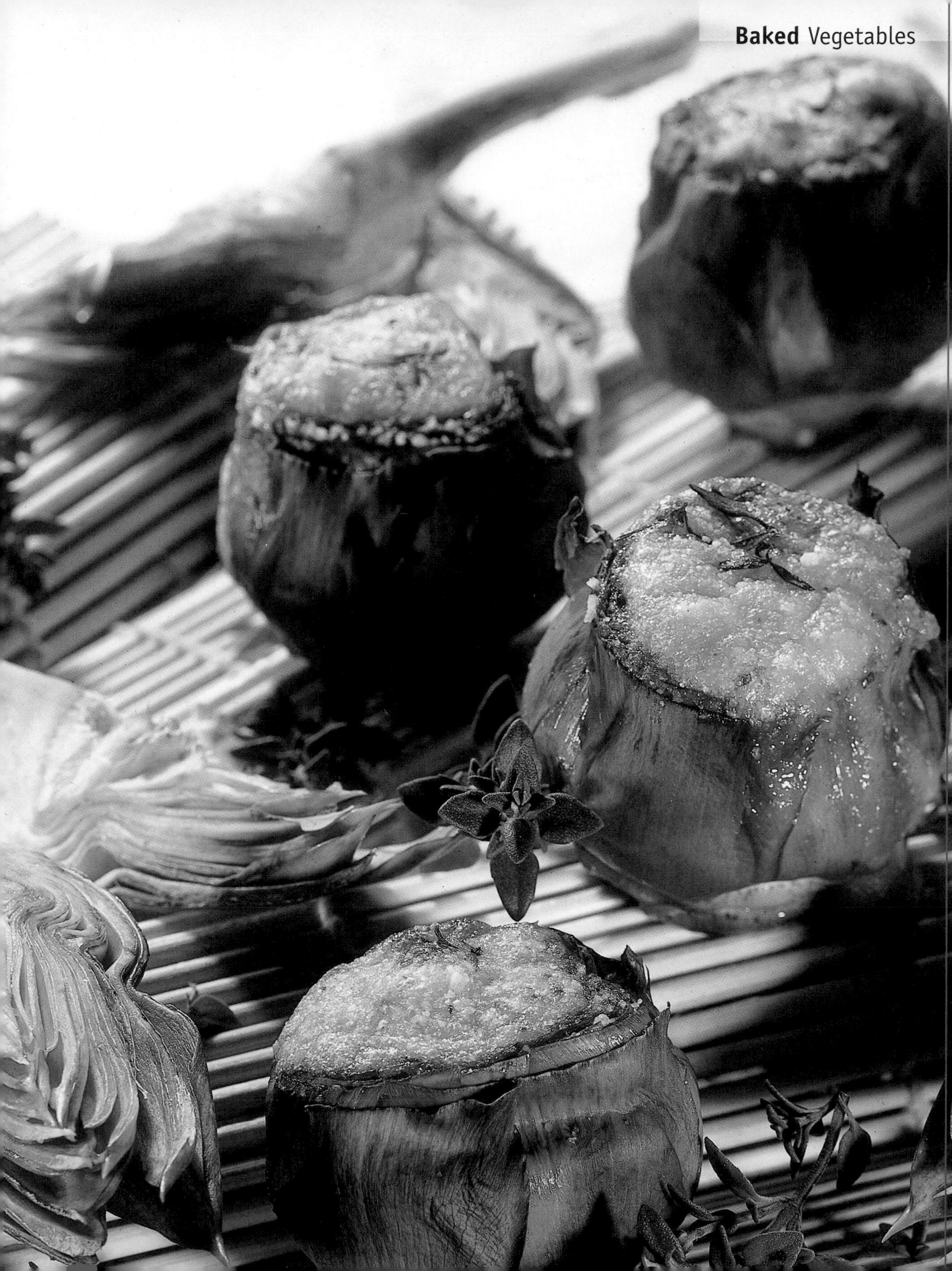

Green Timbales
with Crescenza Cheese Sauce

Serves 4

For the timbales:
⅓ lb (150 g) lettuce
3 egg yolks
3 egg whites
1 cup (250 g) béchamel sauce
1 Tbsp grated parmesan cheese

For the sauce:
1 cup (200 g) crescenza cheese
1 ½ slice (50 g) taleggio cheese
2 Tbsp milk
salt and white pepper

For the ramekins:
½ pat butter
2 Tbsp (10 g) breadcrumbs

Preparation time 20 minutes
Cooking time 40 minutes
Difficulty Easy
Calories 359
Wine Roero Arneis

Wash and dry the lettuce and boil for about 10 minutes in lightly salted boiling water. Drain, leave to cool and squeeze out excess moisture.

1. Blend the lettuce in a food processor with the yolks and pour the mixture into a bowl. Add the parmesan (Picture 1), the thick béchamel sauce and stir.

2. Whisk the egg whites until stiff and add to the lettuce mixture (Picture 2): fold in gently with a whisk (Picture 3).

3. Grease the ramekins, dust with breadcrumbs and fill with the mixture (Picture 4). Arrange in oven dish half filled with water, place in oven and cook for 30 minutes at 350°F (180°C).

4. Cut the taleggio and crescenza into pieces and place in a pan with the milk. Add salt and pepper and melt the cheeses over moderate heat for 5 minutes; stir to avoid lumps. Put the sauce aside.

5. Remove the green timbales from the oven and arrange on plates with the crescenza sauce. Garnish with some fresh lettuce leaves and serve piping hot.

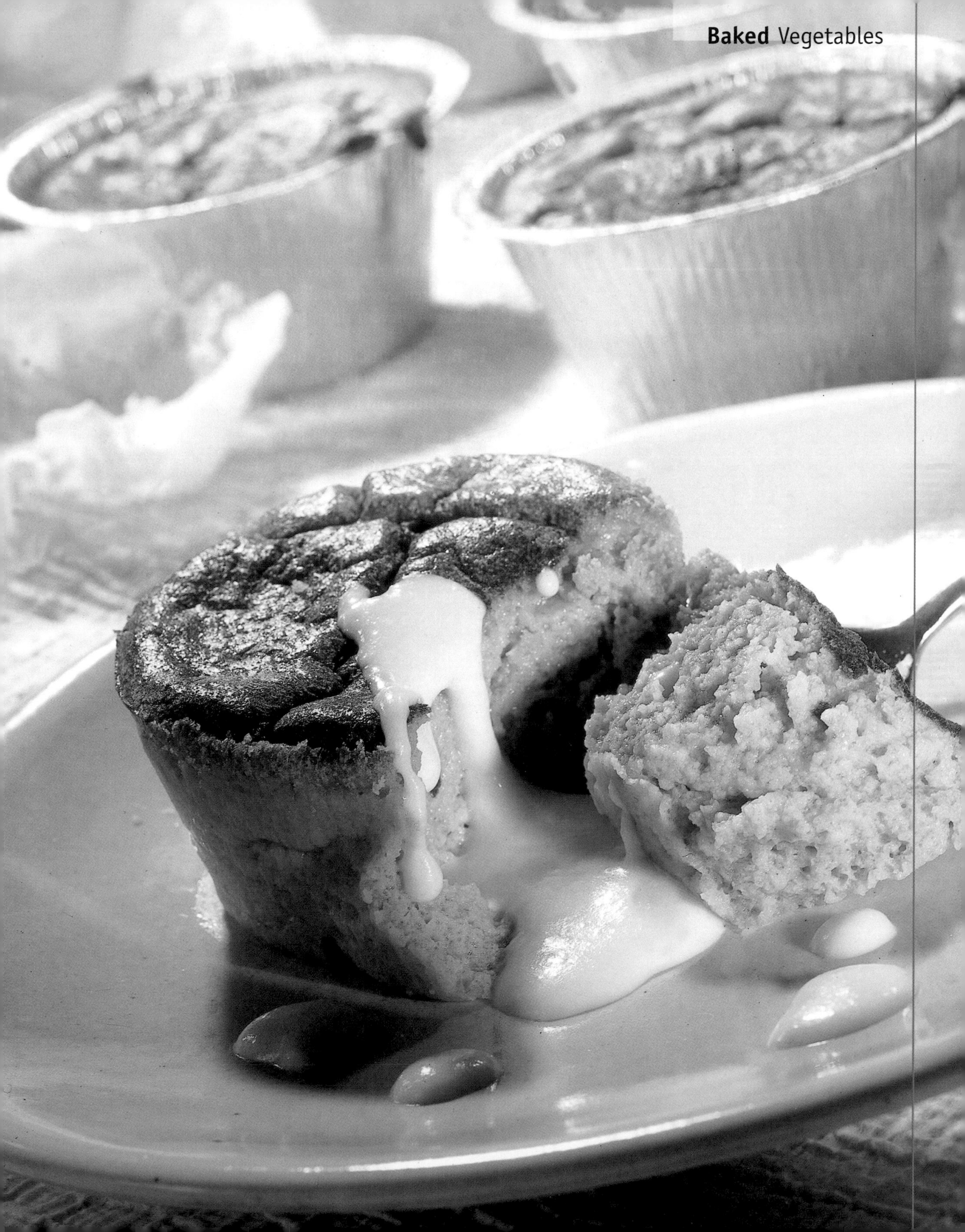

Stuffed Breaded
Artichokes

Serves 4

For the artichokes:
12 Mammola artichokes
1 lemon
1 egg yolk
½ cup (100 g) ricotta cheese
¼ lb (80 g) pecorino cheese
3 slices (30 g) pancetta
salt and pepper

In addition:
1 egg
breadcrumbs
extra-virgin olive oil

Clean the artichokes, discarding all outer leaves and keeping only the tender inner part. Trim the tips of the leaves and remove the stalks. Smear half a lemon over the artichokes to prevent them from darkening.

1. Boil the artichokes in a saucepan with salted water. Drain when firm to the bite, squeeze them lightly to remove excess moisture and leave to dry overturned on a cloth.

2. Blend the ricotta with the pecorino, the egg yolk and the finely chopped pancetta in a bowl. Add salt and pepper. Delicately widen the center of the artichoke hearts and fill completely with the cheese and egg mixture (Picture 1).

3. Dip the stuffed artichokes into the beaten egg (Picture 2) and the breadcrumbs (Picture 3). Arrange the artichokes in a greased oven dish. Drizzle with a little extra-virgin olive oil and bake in oven at 375°F (190°C) for 10 minutes.

4. Serve the stuffed artichokes either warm, hot or cold, as they are suitable for any season and any type of menu.

Preparation time 30 minutes
Cooking time 15 minutes
Difficulty Easy
Calories 390
Wine Marino Superiore

Grilled Eggplant
with Mozzarella and Zucchini

Serves 4

For the vegetables:
⅔ lb (300 g) eggplant
¾ lb (350 g) buffalo mozzarella
¼ lb (200 g) zucchini
⅔ lb (300 g) tomatoes
8 basil leaves
3 Tbsp extra-virgin olive oil

For garnishing:
basil

Peel the eggplant and slice into thin rounds. Grill on both sides on a hot cast-iron griddle and lay on a tray.

1. Thinly slice the zucchini lengthwise and blanch them in lightly salted water for 1 minute. Drain on a tray and leave to cool.

2. Wash the tomatoes in cold water, dry and slice into thin rounds. Cut the buffalo-milk mozzarella into thin slices.

3. Lay the grilled eggplant on a lightly greased oven dish and place 2 slices of boiled zucchini on each eggplant slice (Picture 1). Cover the zucchini with the tomato rounds, add salt and pepper and some basil leaves (Picture 2), the slices of mozzarella and more basil. Cover with another eggplant slice (Picture 3) and top with some mozzarella.

4. Put in hot oven at 350°F (180°C) for approx. 5 minutes. Remove when the mozzarella melts.

5. Garnish the stuffed eggplant with some basil leaves and serve.

Preparation time 30 minutes
Cooking time 15 minutes
Difficulty Easy
Calories 416
Wine Verdicchio di Matelica

1 2 3

Stuffed Zucchini
with Pearled Barley

Serves 4

For the zucchini:

1 lb (450 g) zucchini
1 garlic clove
¾ cup (140 g) pearled barley
¼ lb (70 g) red bell pepper
5-6 thyme sprigs
4 Tbsp extra-virgin olive oil
2 slices (60 g) emmental cheese
salt and pepper

Preparation time 30 minutes
Cooking time 25 minutes
Difficulty Easy
Calories 280
Wine Locorotondo

Boil the pearled barley in salted water for 15 minutes. Drain, rinse under cold water and transfer into a bowl.

1. Clean and trim the zucchini and cut them in half lengthways. Remove the white flesh from the zucchini with a scoop. Chop the zucchini flesh and place the emptied halves in a saucepan of boiling salted water: boil for 3-4 minutes, drain, leave to cool and place on a tray.

2. Clean and cut the red bell pepper into small pieces. Warm the extra-virgin olive oil in a pan and sauté the peeled clove of garlic. Add the diced bell pepper and the zucchini flesh (Picture 1). Sauté, season with salt and pepper and cook for 5 minutes.

3. Add the pearled barley (Picture 2) and cook for 3 minutes. Sprinkle with the finely chopped thyme, stir, remove from heat and add the diced emmental.

4. Stuff the blanched zucchini halves with the barley mixture (Picture 3) and bake gratin in oven for 5 minutes at 350°F (180°C). Distribute the remaining filling on the plates creating a layer of barley and vegetables, arrange the stuffed zucchini on top, dust with some chopped thyme and serve immediately.

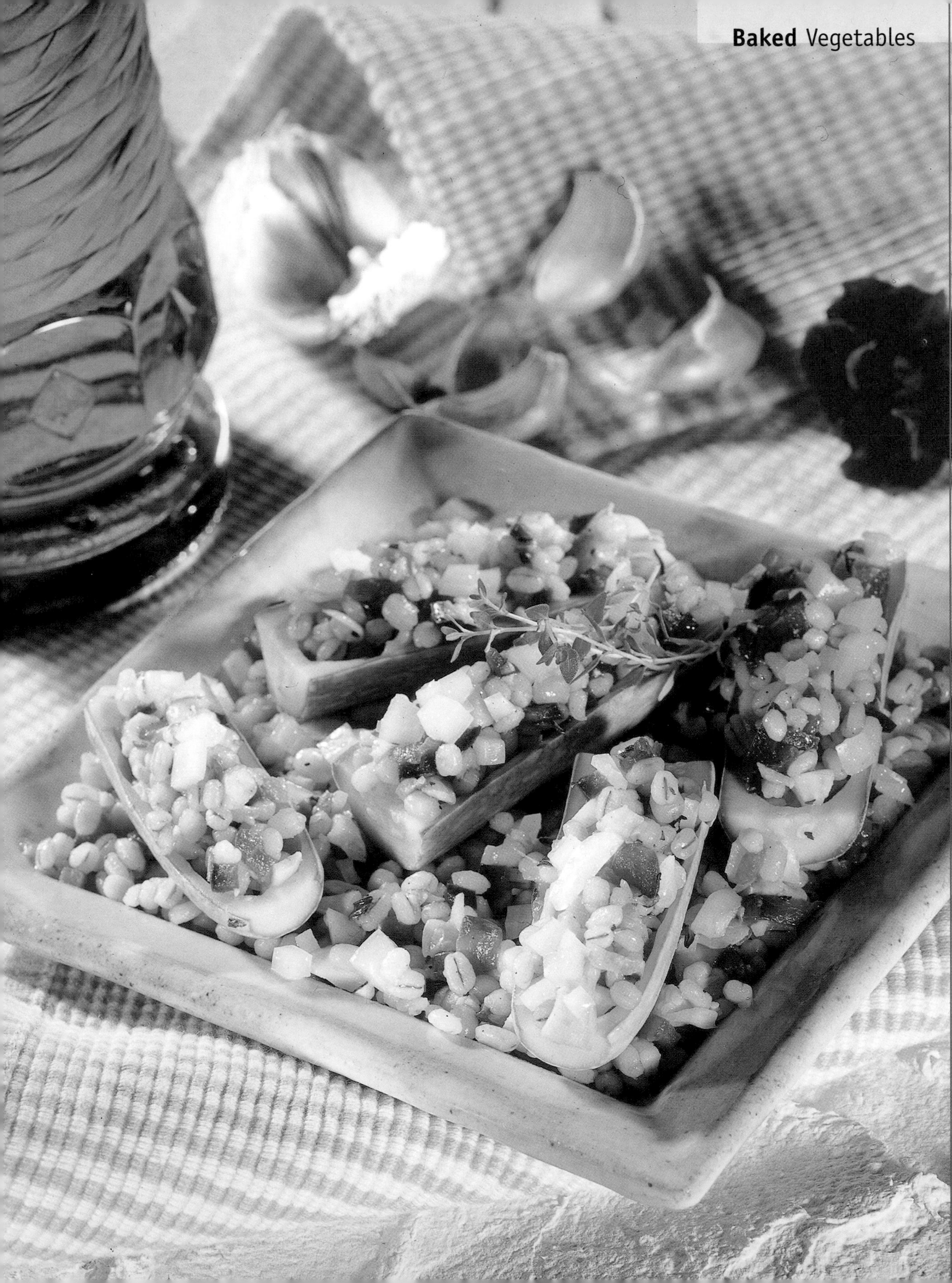

Broccoli Timbales
with Brie Fondue

Serves 6

For the béchamel sauce:
1 ¼ cups (300 ml) milk
2 pats butter
3 Tbsp (30 g) all-purpose flour
salt

For the timbales:
½ lb (220 g) broccoli
¼ lb (120 g) scamorza cheese
5 Tbsp grated parmesan cheese
2 egg yolks
2 egg whites
fennel seeds
salt

For the brie fondue:
¾ lb (150 g) brie
1 ⅓ cups (350 ml) milk
1 Tbsp (10 g) potato starch
1 egg yolk
salt

Preparation time 40 minutes
Cooking time 50 minutes
Difficulty Medium
Calories 333
Wine Bardolino Chiaretto

Melt the butter in a saucepan, add the flour and mix until it starts to simmer. Pour the milk in and bring to the boil until the béchamel sauce thickens. Remove the saucepan from heat and salt to taste.

1. Clean the broccoli and boil them for 5-6 minutes in salted water. Pour the béchamel sauce into a bowl, add the parmesan, diced scamorza, pieces of broccoli and yolks. Season with salt and add the chopped fennel seeds.

2. Warm the oven at 350°F (170°C). Place an oven dish half filled with water inside the oven. Add the whipped egg whites to the broccoli mixture (Picture 1) and fold in gently (Picture 2). Grease the ramekins, fill with the mixture (Picture 3) and place on the oven dish. Cook at 350°F (170°C) for approx. 30 minutes.

3. In the meantime, break the brie into pieces and discard the white rind; place it in a saucepan with ¾ of the milk and a pinch of salt and bring to a boil.

4. Mix the potato starch with the remaining milk: once the brie has melted, add the potato starch and milk mixture. Stir and, when the mixture starts to bubble, remove from heat, add the egg yolk and blend.

5. Arrange a timbale in each plate and serve with the hot brie fondue.

110

Sautéed Lentils
with Wild Rice

Serves 4

For the lentils

¾ cup (150 g) lentils
1 garlic clove
1 shallot
3 Tbsp extra-virgin olive oil
¾ cup (200 g) tomato purée
salt and pepper
2 Tbsp parsley

For the rice:

½ cup (100 g) Arborio rice
¾ cup (100 g) wild rice
2 (300 g) red bell pepper
3 Tbsp extra-virgin olive oil
¼ lb (100 g) smoked scamorza cheese

Place the lentils in a bowl, cover with plenty of cold water and leave to rest for approx. 2 hours. Boil the two varieties of rice for 15-18 minutes in lightly salted boiling water, drain and put aside.

1. Peel the red pepper and dice. Sauté the bell pepper in a pan with the oil, add the rice and fry lightly for approx. 4 minutes over medium heat. Remove from heat and keep warm.

2. Boil the lentils for approx. 20-25 minutes in plenty of salted water. Drain and leave in the colander. Place the chopped shallot, the crushed clove of garlic and the oil in a pan and cook well.

3. Add the boiled lentils to the pan with the shallot (Picture 1) and the tomato purée (Picture 2). Season with a little salt and pepper and cook for 10 minutes over moderate heat, stirring frequently. Once the ingredients are cooked, add the chopped parsley.

4. Spread out the rice and bell pepper in oven dish, add the lentils and scatter thin strips of scamorza over the surface. Place in a hot oven at 350°F (180°C) for 5-10 minutes and serve immediately.

Preparation time 30 minutes
Cooking time 55 minutes
Difficulty Easy
Calories 450
Wine Cerveteri Bianco

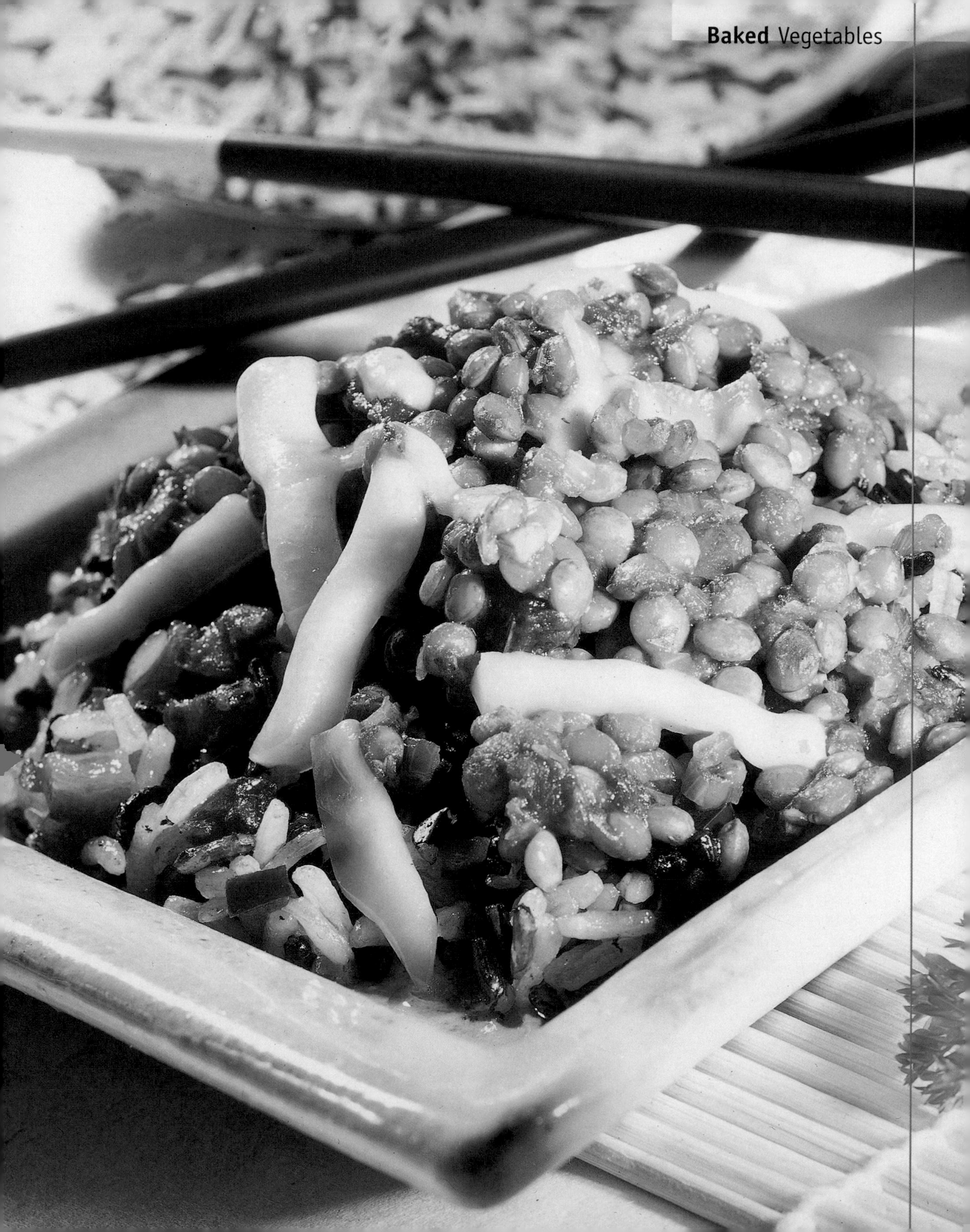

Stuffed Artichokes
with Vegetables and Chickpeas

Serves 6

For the artichokes:

8 artichokes
1 green onion
¼ lb (130 g) carrots
⅓ lb (150 g) zucchini
¼ lb (120 g) canned chickpeas
3 Tbsp extra-virgin olive oil
1 garlic clove
1 small bunch of chives
½ lb (100 g) emmental cheese
5 Tbsp grated parmesan cheese
salt and pepper

Preparation time 25 minutes
Cooking time 15 minutes
Difficulty Easy
Calories 179
Wine Roero Arneis

Cut the stalk from the artichokes at 1 ¼-1 ½ in (3-4 cm) from the flower bud, remove the thorns with a knife and discard the tougher outer leaves. Peel the rest of the stalk (Picture 1) and cut the artichoke flower buds into halves. Remove the choke and some of the inner leaves with a scoop so as to form a cavity (Picture 2).

1. Blanch the artichokes in lightly salted water for approx. 3 minutes, drain well and arrange on a tray.

2. Clean the onion and slice it into rounds. Wash the carrots and the zucchini and dice finely. Sauté the onion in a pan with the garlic and oil; shortly after, add the zucchini and carrots, season with salt and pepper and cook for 3-4 minutes.

3. Drain the chickpeas from their water, add to the pan and continue to cook for approx. 2 minutes. Dust with the finely chopped chives.

4. Stuff the artichokes with the vegetable mixture (Picture 3) and place on an oven tray. Scatter the diced emmental over the artichokes, dust with grated parmesan and put in oven.

5. Bake the artichokes au gratin at 350°F (180°C) for 5 minutes. Remove from oven when the cheese has completely melted, dust with another sprinkle of parmesan and serve immediately.

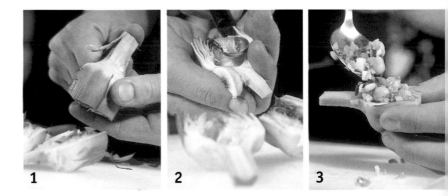

1   2   3

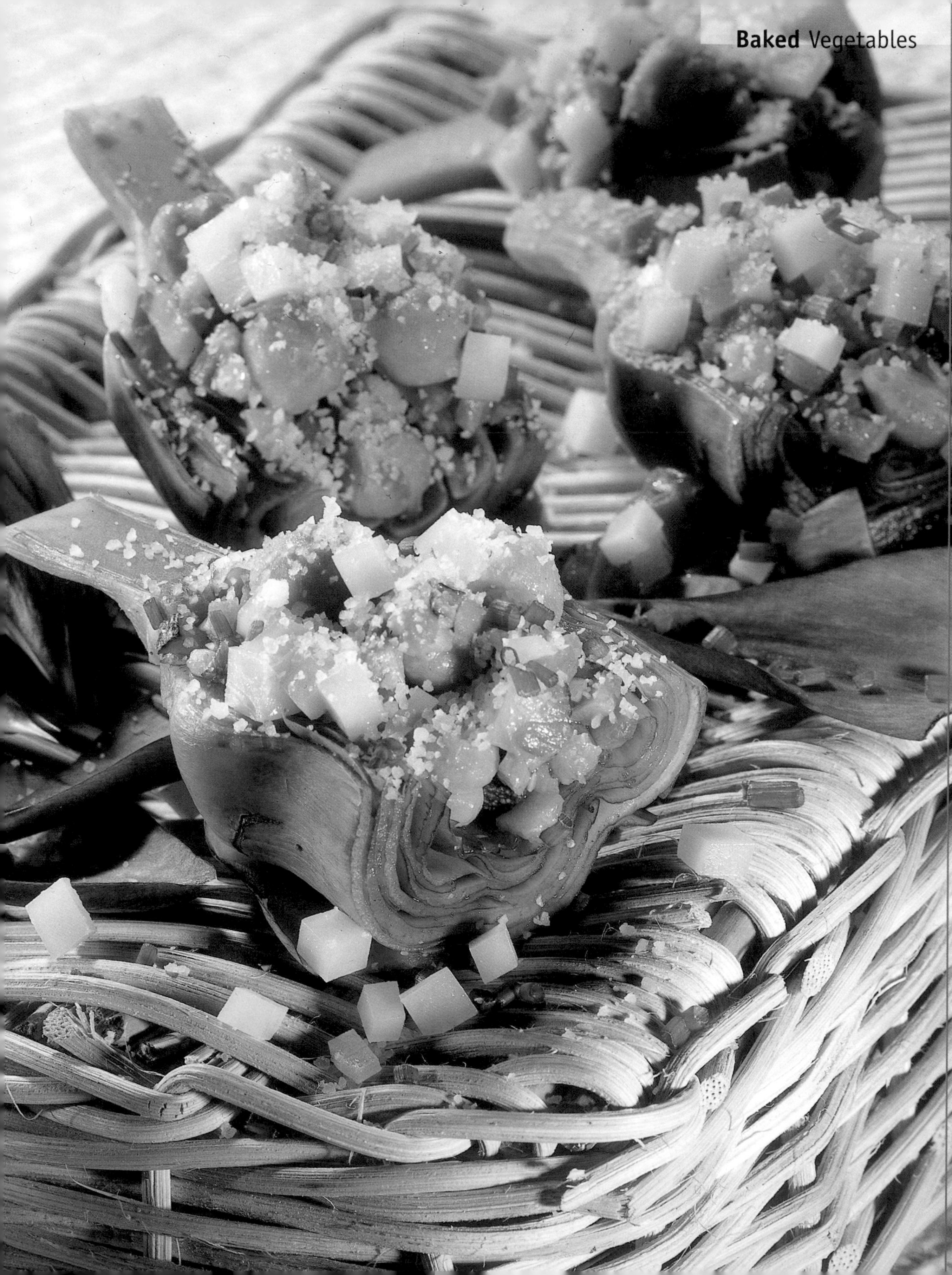

Vegetable Roll
with Pumpkin Cream

Serves 6

For the roll:
¾ lb (350 g) fresh spinach
3 carrots
½ stalk celery
¼ shallot
6 Tbsp grated parmesan cheese
1 egg
3 Tbsp extra-virgin olive oil
2 Tbsp (10 g) breadcrumbs
salt and pepper

For the filling:
1 ⅓ cups (250 g) fresh ricotta cheese
1 egg
5 Tbsp grated parmesan cheese
nutmeg
salt

For the pumpkin cream:
½ lb (220 g) pumpkin flesh
⅔ lb (150 ml) fresh cream
⅓ cup (100 ml) water
salt and pepper

Preparation time 40 minutes
Cooking time 30 minutes
Difficulty Medium
Calories 307
Wine Lugana

Boil the spinach for 2 minutes in salted water, drain, leave to cool and squeeze out excess water. Clean and dice the carrots, the celery and the shallot. Sauté the diced vegetables in a pan with the oil over moderate heat. Chop the spinach and blend in 1 egg, the parmesan, the sautéed vegetables, and some salt and pepper. Stir and put aside.

1. Mix the ricotta with the egg, parmesan, some salt and grated nutmeg. Roll out a sheet of kitchen foil: grease and dust it with the breadcrumbs. Roll out the spinach mixture to form an ½ in (1 cm) thick layer.

2. Spread the ricotta filling on the vegetable mixture (Picture 1), and roll it up in kitchen foil (Picture 2), pressing the edges firmly to close. Bake at 350°F (180°C) for 25 minutes and leave to cool in the refrigerator.

3. Dice the pumpkin and place in a saucepan with the cream, water, salt and pepper. Cook over moderate heat for 10 minutes, remove from heat and blend all the ingredients together into a sauce.

4. Take the firmed roll, slice into ½ in (1 cm) thick rounds and arrange on plates with a heaped Tbsp of hot pumpkin cream.

1   2

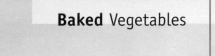

Fennel and Ham au Gratin
with Brie Sauce

Serves 4

For the fennels:
2 ¼ lb (1 kg) fennels
½ lemon
salt

For the brie sauce:
1 ¼ cups (300 ml) milk
2 pats butter
2 Tbsp (20 g) all-purpose flour
½ lb (180 g) brie
salt

For baking au gratin:
3 slices (100 g) cooked ham
⅕ lb (50 g) brie

Preparation time 30 minutes
Cooking time 20 minutes
Difficulty Medium
Calories 438
Wine Nebbiolo d'Alba

Clean the fennels, discarding the green feathery leaves and the outer layer, and cut into wedges (Picture 1). Squeeze the ½ lemon and keep the juice aside.

1. Bring a saucepan of lightly salted water to the boil, add the lemon juice and boil the fennels; drain when firm to the bite (after about 4-5 minutes), place on a tray and leave to cool.

2. Melt the butter in a saucepan, add the flour (Picture 2) and stir until lump free. When the mixture starts to simmer, pour in the milk (Picture 3), mix with a whisk and add the pieces of brie, free from its white rind. Bring the fondue to the boil stirring constantly: lightly season with salt and, after 2-3 minutes, remove from heat.

3. Lightly grease a ceramic oven dish and place the fennel inside; smother with the brie sauce. Add thin strips of ham (Picture 4) and some pieces of brie with its white rind.

4. Place the oven dish in a hot oven at 375°F (190°C) and bake au gratin for 10-15 minutes until the surface is golden. Serve immediately.

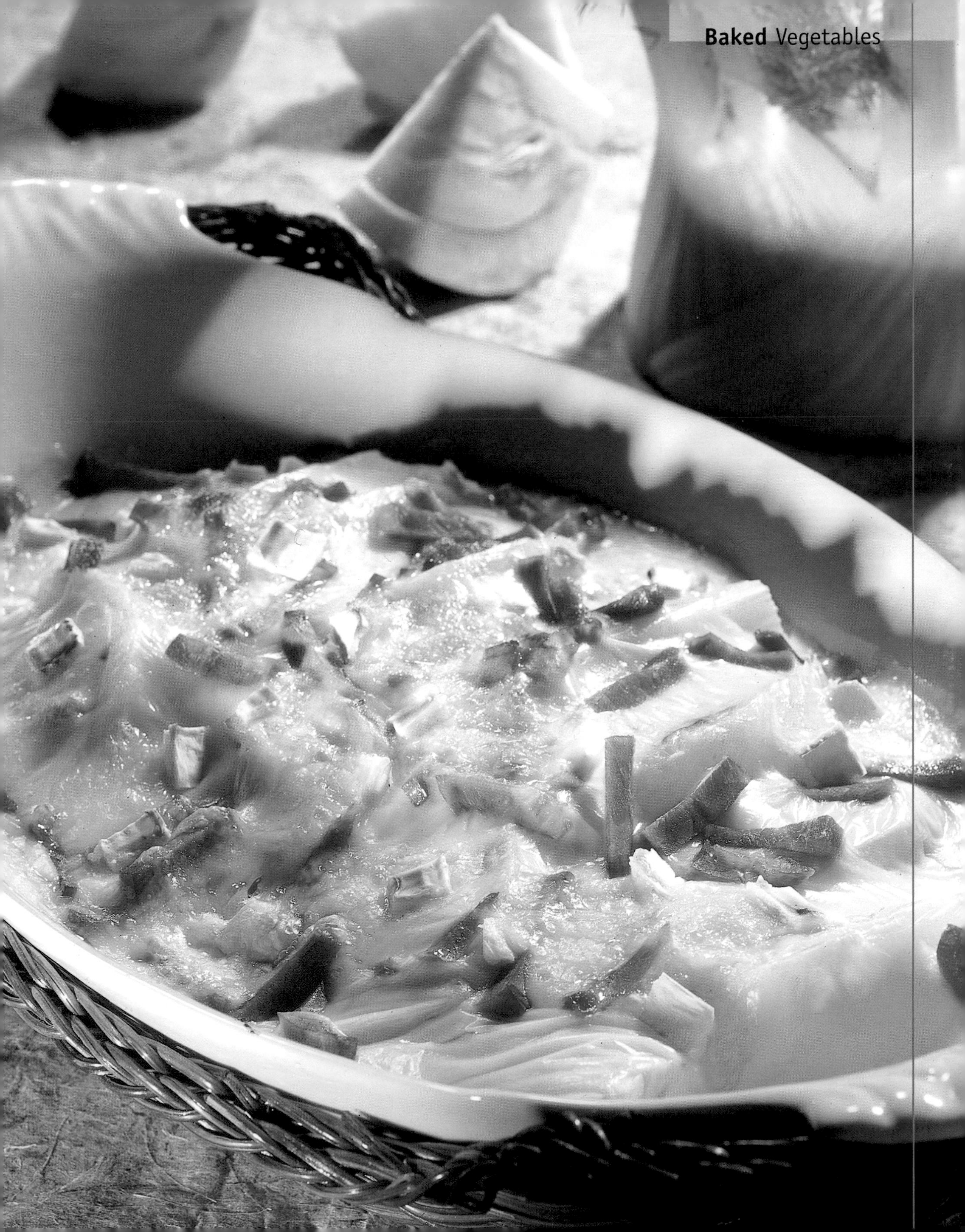

Chickpea Cannelloni
with Leek and Pumpkin Filling

Serves 4

For the cannelloni pastry:
1 ½ cups (200 g) all-purpose flour
1 ⅓ cups (100 g) semolina flour
¾ cup (100 g) chickpea flour
4 eggs
1 Tbsp extra-virgin olive oil

For the filling:
⅔ lb (300 g) pumpkin
½ leek
5 Tbsp grated parmesan cheese
⅓ cup macaroons
1 egg
salt, pepper and nutmeg
6 Tbsp extra-virgin olive oil
vegetable broth
¼ cup Marsala wine

For the broccoli sauce:
¾ lb (150 g) broccoli
1 garlic clove
2 unsalted anchovies
ice
1 Tbsp corn starch
4 Tbsp extra-virgin olive oil
½ shallot
salt and pepper

For the vegetables:
1 zucchini
1 carrot
½ fennel
1 small stalk celery
¾ cup (200 ml) extra-virgin olive oil
1 handful string beans
½ bell peppers
1 small bunch herbs sugar

½ tsp saffron
salt and pepper

For baking au gratin:
1 pat butter
parmesan cheese

Work the ingredients for the pastry together, roll out into a sheet and cut out some rectangles; boil the pastry rectangles for 1 minute and drain on a cloth.

1. Slice the leek and simmer in a pan with oil and butter, add the pumpkin (Picture 1) and the Marsala. Add the crumbled macaroons (Picture 2), salt and pepper; cook until the pumpkin has softened completely (add broth if it sticks). Pass the mixture through a vegetable mill and incorporate the egg, cheese, nutmeg and salt.

2. Blanch the broccoli and sauté in a pan with 2 Tbsp of oil (Picture 3), the chopped shallot and the garlic; put in a container with the anchovies, some ice, the remaining oil and the corn starch and process with an immersion blender. Season to taste.

3. Using the water used to cook the broccoli, quickly blanch the diced vegetables and then sauté them in a pan with oil, saffron and the herbs; season with salt and leave to rest for 30 minutes.

4. Fill the pastry rectangles with the pumpkin mixture; close them and bake au gratin for 10 minutes at 350°F (160°C) after brushing them with butter and parmesan.

5. Pour the hot broccoli sauce on the plates, arrange the cannelloni and finish off with the vegetables.

Preparation time 45 minutes
Cooking time 30 minutes
Difficulty Medium
Calories 820
Wine Ribolla Gialla

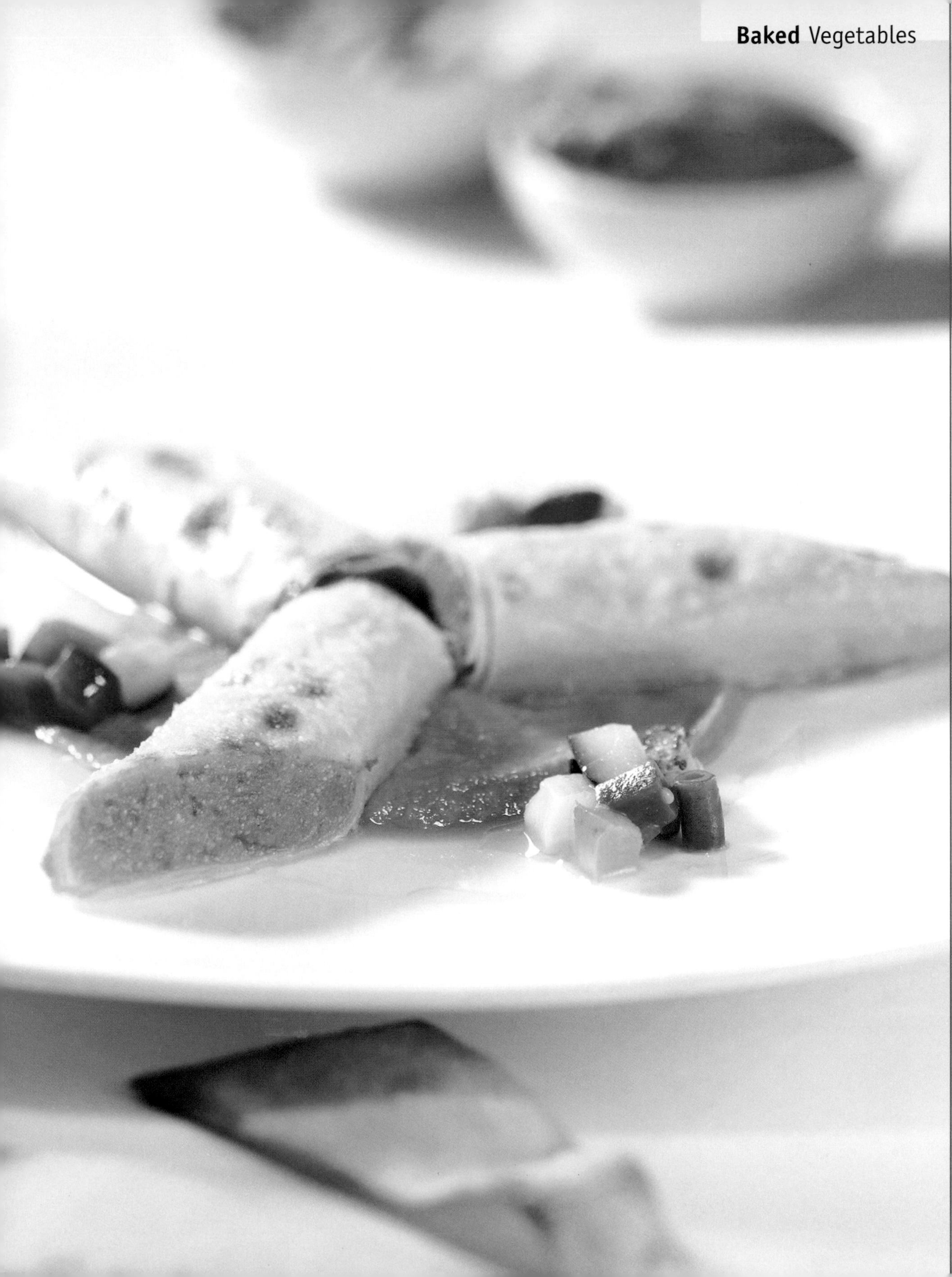

Vegetables **in Salad**

Salad with Robiola Cheese
and Bell Peppers

Serves 4

For the salad:
½ red bell pepper
½ yellow bell pepper
1 lettuce heart
¾ cup (150 g) robiola cheese
1 small eggplant
2 Tbsp almonds
salt and pepper

For the dressing
extra-virgin olive oil
salt and pepper

Char the bell peppers over a low flame without burning excessively (Picture 1). Place in a plastic bag and leave to steam for a few minutes. Peel and cut into strips (Picture 2).

1. Wash and dice the eggplant. Sauté in a non-stick pan with some extra-virgin olive oil and season with salt and pepper.

2. Wash and dry the lettuce, julienne it and arrange on plates.

3. Slice the almonds and toast them in a non-stick pan. Add the lettuce with the bell peppers, the pieces of robiola cheese and the warm diced eggplant. Dress to taste and serve.

Kitchen tip Use the same ingredients to prepare some delicious rollups: cut the eggplant into thin slices, grill and stuff with strips of bell peppers, lettuce, toasted almonds and robiola; roll up the eggplant slices and close with some chive stems. For more flavor, marinate the rollups in some basil-flavored oil.

Preparation time 15 minutes
Difficulty Easy
Calories 159
Wine Alto Adige Müller Thurgau

White Salad with Cuttlefish,
Tomatoes and Sautéed Fava Beans

Serves 4

For the tomatoes:

3 Marzano tomatoes
½ lb (200 g) fresh fava beans
1 lb (450 g) cuttlefish
2 garlic cloves

For the dressing:

6 Tbsp extra-virgin olive oil
oregano
salt and pepper

Wash the tomatoes, cut into thin slices and dust the with oregano. Shell the fava beans and remove the skin (Picture 1).

1. Warm the garlic cloves in a pan and simmer the fava beans for 25 minutes, adding a little water.

2. Boil the cleaned cuttlefish in lightly salted water and drain as soon as they are cooked (8-10 minutes).

3. Scald the slices of tomato on a griddle (Picture 2) or in an oven with a little oil, salt and pepper and arrange on plates. Cover with the stewed fava beans and season with salt and pepper.

4. Add the diced cuttlefish and dress with some oil, oregano, salt and pepper.

Kitchen tip Prepare a cuttlefish salad with boiled potatoes, walnuts or pine nuts. Cook the cuttlefish in a pressure cooker for 30 minutes and cut into pieces. Boil the same amount of potatoes and stir with some Tbsps of walnuts and pine nuts until well blended. Dress with plenty of oil, salt and parsley.

Preparation time 20 minutes
Cooking time 15 minutes
Difficulty Medium
Calories 227
Wine Sicilia Chardonnay

Salad with Bell Peppers,
Onion and Parmesan

Serves 4

For the salad:

1 cup lettuce

1 can corn

2 green onions

1 piece (150 g) parmesan cheese

½ red bell pepper

For the dressing:

extra-virgin olive oil

salt and pepper

Gently wash the lettuce and dry well. Wash the bell pepper, remove the seeds and the white parts and cut into strips.

1. Remove the roots from the green onions and slice into thin rounds.

2. Drain the water from the can and rinse the corn; add to the corn salad, bell pepper and green onions.

3. Dress the salad to taste with the extra-virgin olive oil (better if with a fruity aroma), season with salt and pepper and top with strips of cheese.

Kitchen tip It is always better to use lemon instead of vinegar for dressing corn salad. Add flavor and make the salad easier to digest by cooking the bell pepper with its skin on in a cast iron griddle or in an oven, placing it in a plastic bag to steam for 20 minutes, and peel the skin off by hand. Once the skin is removed, slice into strips and add to the salad.

Preparation time 10 minutes
Difficulty Easy
Calories 237
Wine Alto Adige Pinot Bianco

Spring Salad
with Crab Meat

Serves 4

For the salad:
4 slices of white canapé bread
1 egg
1 Tbsp milk
½ lb (200 g) crab meat in brine
4 tomatoes
2 baby carrots
2 small zucchini
extra-virgin olive oil

For the dressing:
2 Tbsp extra-virgin olive oil
parsley
½ lemon
salt and pepper

For garnishing:
parsley

Preparation time 20 minutes
Cooking time 2 minutes
Difficulty Easy
Calories 349
Wine Lugana

Wash the tomatoes, zucchini, carrots and parsley. Drain the brine from the canned crab meat and rinse under cold water.

1. Cut the tomatoes into wedges, slice the carrots into thin strips (Picture 1) and chop the parsley. Trim the zucchini and slice them thinly with a mandolin slicer (Picture 2) or with a sharp knife.

2. Stir all the ingredients in a bowl until well blended and dress with oil, salt and pepper, parsley and lemon juice.

3. Cut 4 circles out of the bread slices using a round cutter. Beat the egg in a bowl with the milk and a little salt. Dip the bread in the beaten egg and toast until golden in a non-stick pan with a little oil (Picture 3).

4. Serve the crab salad on the hot toasted bread rounds, using a round cutter to arrange it neatly (Picture 4). Decorate with some parsley leaves.

Kitchen tip For a stronger and more sophisticated flavor, replace the crab meat with smoked Norwegian salmon; slice the salmon into thin strips and dress as indicated by this recipe, using wild fennel or dill instead of parsley.

Oriental Salad
with Red Cabbage

Serves 4

For the salad:
1 head lettuce
2 zucchini
10 cherry tomatoes
¼ red cabbage

For the dressing:
extra-virgin olive oil
soy sauce (shoyu)

Wash the lettuce thoroughly and dry well in a salad spinner.

1. Clean the tomatoes and cut into pieces (Picture 1). Trim the zucchini and slice into matchsticks.

2. Remove the outer leaves of the red cabbage and slice finely.

3. Julienne the lettuce (Picture 2) and arrange the salad in the plates; dress with oil and soy sauce. Soy sauce can be replaced with 3 tablespoons of balsamic vinegar.

Kitchen tip Cook the finely sliced red cabbage in a hot pan with extra-virgin olive oil and 1 unpeeled clove of garlic. Dilute some soy sauce with 2 tablespoons of water and sprinkle over the cabbage. Leave to soften over the heat for 5-6 minutes. Serve cold with the lettuce and the other ingredients.

Preparation time 20 minutes
Difficulty Easy
Calories 170
Wine Riesling Renano

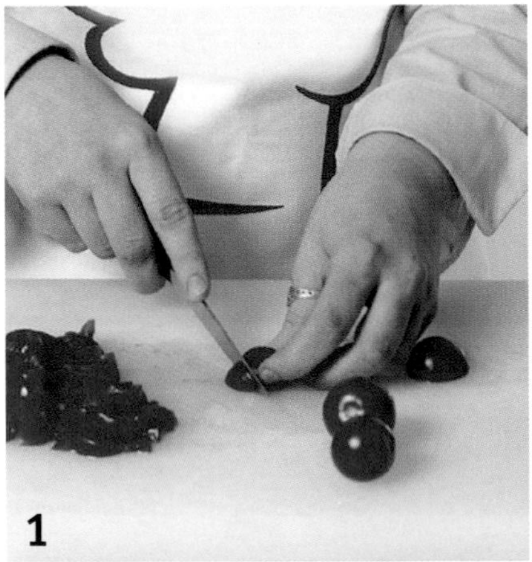

1

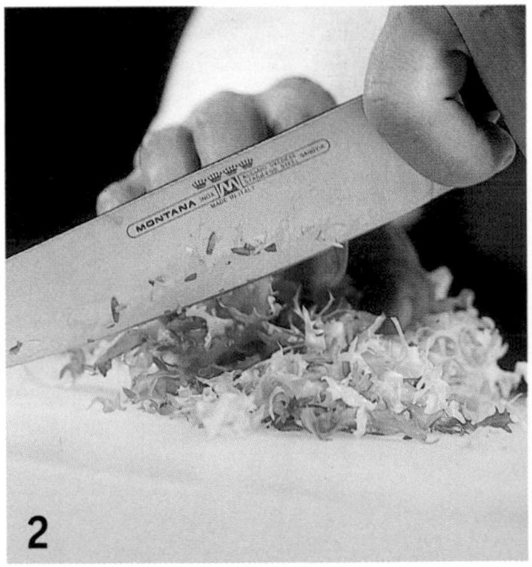

2

Salad with Bresaola
in Blueberry Vinaigrette

Serves 4

For the salad:
½ lb (200 g) thickly sliced bresaola
⅔ cup (120 g) green lentils
1 head frisee lettuce

For the vinaigrette:
7 Tbsp mild extra-virgin olive oil
½ cup (100 g) blueberries
2 cloves garlic
1 tsp balsamic vinegar
salt and pepper

Wash the lentils thoroughly by placing them in a sieve under running water.

1. Place the lentils in a saucepan with the unpeeled cloves of garlic, cold water and salt. Cook for approx. 30 minutes and leave to cool in their water.

2. Thoroughly wash the salad, strip the leaves off and dry with a clean cloth.

3. Prepare the vinaigrette by pureeing the blueberries with oil, vinegar, salt and pepper. Julienne the bresaola and keep in a cool place.

4. Tear the lettuce leaves, arrange on plates and scatter the julienned bresaola on top. Surround with the warm lentils and dress with the vinaigrette and some blueberries.

Kitchen tip For a touch of class, use venison bresaola or beef fillet carpaccio. Add more flavor by using some lightly smoked meat: slice thinly and serve with the other ingredients in the salad.

Preparation time 15 minutes
Cooking time 30 minutes
Difficulty Easy
Calories 285
Wine Valcalepio Rosso

Salad with Carrots,
Feta Cheese and Cherry Tomatoes

Serves 4

For the salad:
1 small bunch of lettuce
1 small bunch red mesclun
4 baby carrots
1 cup feta cheese
15 cherry tomatoes
2 slices rye bread

For the dressing:
3 Tbsp mild extra-virgin olive oil
salt and pepper

Wash the lettuce and the red mesclun and dry well in a salad spinner.

1. Peel and julienne the carrots (Picture 1) and place in cold water. Wash the tomatoes and cut into quarters.

2. Dice the bread and toast it in a non-stick pan with a small amount of extra-virgin olive oil.

3. Make the salad by mixing all the ingredients and topping with the diced cheese. Dress with the mild extra-virgin olive oil, season with salt and pepper and serve.

Interesting to know Rye bread has a distinct and sour flavor, a compact texture and a thin and hard crust. It is often flavored with caraway seeds or fennel. It keeps fresh for a few days.

Preparation time 20 minutes
Cooking time 3 minutes
Difficulty Easy
Calories 275
Wine Friuli Collio Chardonnay

1

Quick Mixed
Vegetable Salad

Serves 4

For the salad:
2 cucumbers
1 small bunch radishes
²/₃ lb (300 g) carrots
2 stalks green celery
1 small Chinese cabbage
1 small bunch wild arugula
2 Tbsp coarse salt

For the dressing:
extra-virgin olive oil
lemon juice or rice vinegar

Clean all the vegetables, slice the carrots, the radishes and the cucumbers into thin rounds, the celery into diagonal slices and the Chinese cabbage into strips.

1. Arrange the prepared vegetables in layers in a tall and narrow jar (or in a vegetable press), separating the layers with ground coarse salt. Cover with a plate with a diameter that is smaller than the top of the jar and place a weight on top.

2. Leave to rest overnight, then remove the extracted liquid and serve the vegetables mixed with the shredded arugula.

3. Dress the salad with the extra-virgin olive oil and some drops of lemon juice or rice vinegar to taste.

Kitchen tip This recipe can be used as a base to give flavor to a number of vegetable dishes, enhancing their flavor and adding dietary minerals. Excellent vegetable main courses can be created by adding other ingredients such as fresh cheese, hard-boiled eggs, mushroom carpaccio, etc.

Preparation time 15 minutes
Difficulty Easy
Calories 85
Wine Verdiso dei Colli Trevigiani

New Panzanella
Salad

Serves 4

For the Panzanella:
8 slices bread
2 green onions
2 asparagus
2 tomatoes
2 young zucchini

For the dressing:
6 Tbsp extra-virgin olive oil
balsamic vinegar
basil
salt and pepper

Trim the zucchini and blanch in salted water for 2 minutes; leave to cool. Wash the tomatoes and dice them discarding the seeds (Picture 1). Peel and blanch the asparagus. Clean the green onions and slice into rounds.

1. Slice the bread (preferably homemade) and dice; toast quickly in an oven or in a non-stick pan with a little oil, salt and pepper.

2. Place the tomatoes, chopped zucchini, asparagus and green onions in a bowl. Dress the salad with oil and balsamic vinegar (Picture 2). Add the bread, mix well and season with some shredded basil (Picture 3).

3. Fill 4 ramekins and leave to rest in the refrigerator before serving.

Kitchen tip For the traditional panzanella recipe, soak some stale bread in water and vinegar, then squeeze out the liquid and crumble by hand. Add some mixed summer vegetables with 1 thinly sliced red onion and plenty of basil; dress with extra-virgin olive oil, salt and pepper.

Preparation time 30 minutes
Cooking time 15 minutes
Difficulty Easy
Calories 341
Wine Morellino di Scansano

Warm Artichoke Salad
with Ham and Pecorino Cheese

Serves 4

For the salad:
4 artichokes
2 cardoon stems
½ lb (200 g) broccoli
1 small bunch marjoram
1 small bunch parsley
¾ cup (200 ml) milk
½ lb (200 g) thinly sliced Parma ham
⅔ lb (150 g) mature pecorino cheese
1 garlic clove

For the dressing:
5 Tbsp extra-virgin olive oil
salt and pepper

Clean the artichokes by removing the outer leaves and the stalk. Trim (Picture 1-2) and remove the internal choke. Put the artichoke hearts in a pot with a clove of garlic and some marjoram and parsley. Cover with water, add salt and cook until tender but not falling apart.

1. Remove the fibrous strings from the cardoons, chop into pieces approx. 2 in (3 cm) long and cook in the milk, diluted with ¾ cup (200 ml) of water, and a pinch of salt for 30 minutes.

2. Divide the broccoli into florets and cook for 5 minutes in boiling salted water.

3. Drain all the vegetables from their cooking liquid and place in a bowl, after having cut the artichokes in quarters.

4. Dress the vegetables with oil, salt and pepper, lay in the center of the plate, surround with the slices of prosciutto and dust with shavings of pecorino.

Kitchen tip Cardoons are similar to artichokes and tend to darken rather quickly; for this reason it is important, after it has been sliced, to preserve the cardoon in water and lemon or rub it rapidly with a lemon.

Preparation time 45 minutes
Cooking time 45 minutes
Difficulty Easy
Calories 418
Wine Est! Est!! Est!!!

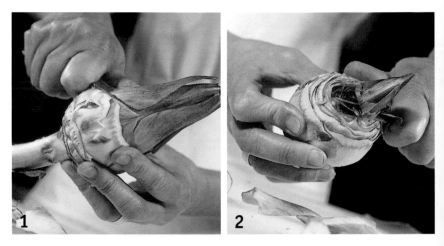

Calabria-style
Bean Casserole

Serves 4

For the Calabria-style beans:
¾ cup (150 g) dried pinto beans
1 red bell pepper
1 yellow bell pepper
1 red onion
2 large potatoes
2 garlic cloves
2 bay leaves

For the dressing:
1 small bunch parsley
1 pinch dried oregano
4 Tbsp extra-virgin olive oil
chili pepper
salt and pepper

P repare the dried beans by soaking them overnight. Once softened, cook the beans in a saucepan with cold water, the bay leaves and a pinch of salt for approx. 40 minutes.

1. Thinly slice the onion (Picture 1) and fry lightly in a saucepan with the oil and the cloves of garlic.

2. Wash and cut the bell peppers into pieces, peel and cut the potatoes into large pieces and add the vegetables to the pan with the onion.

3. Drain the beans with a skimmer and add them, while still hot, to the vegetables; season with salt and pepper and cook for approx. 30 minutes, adding some of the water in which the vegetables were cooked in from time to time.

4. Dust with the chopped parsley, oregano and chili pepper to taste. Leave to gain flavor for a few more minutes and serve the Calabria-style beans with slices of rustic wheat bread.

Kitchen tip Use precooked beans to speed up the preparation. In this case, drain the beans, rinse under cold water, add to the vegetables and continue from step 3.

Preparation time 1 hour and
                                            15 minutes
Cooking time 25 minutes
Difficulty Medium
Calories 255
Wine Cirò Rosato

1

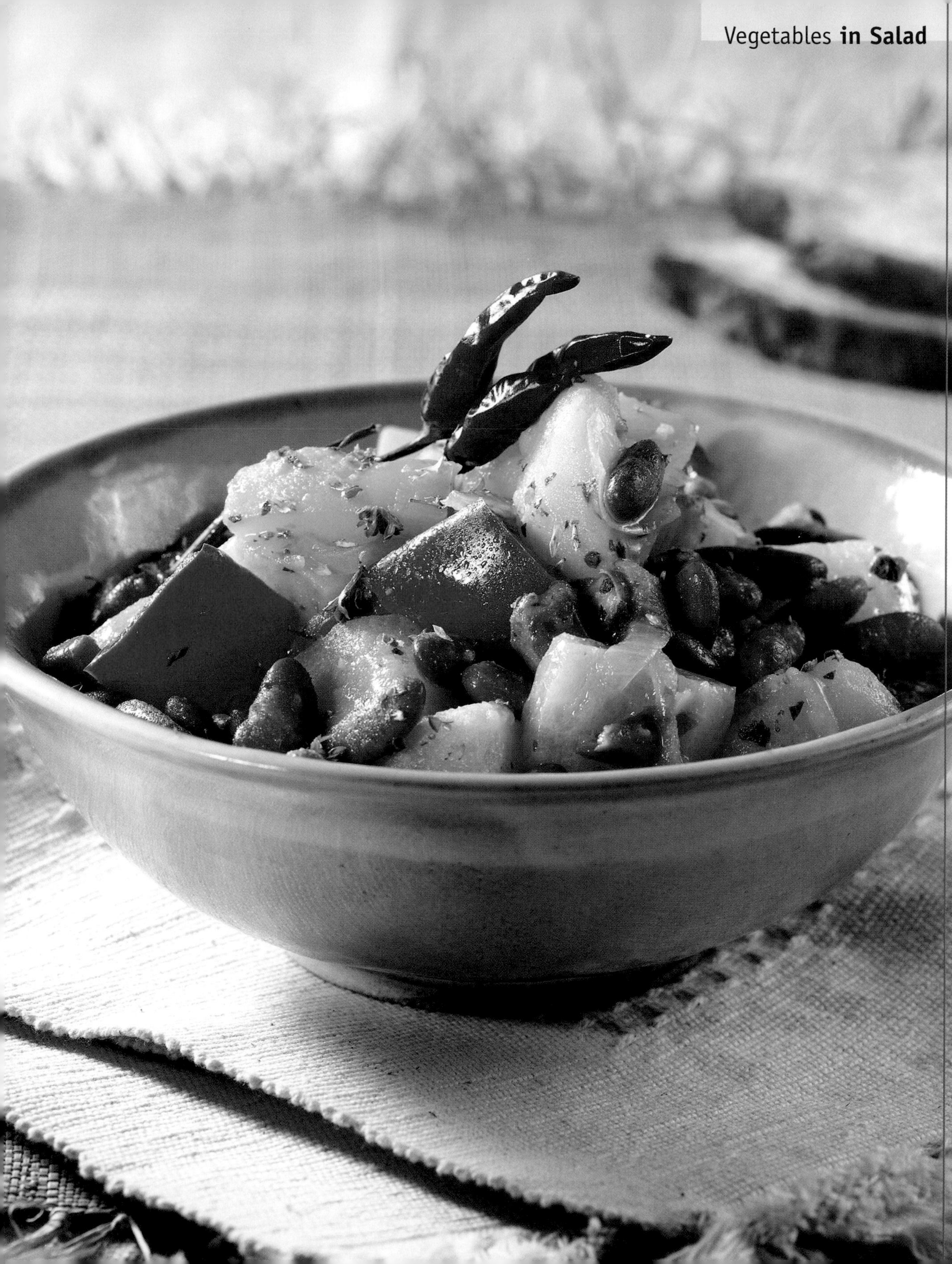

Stuffed Tomatoes
with Tuna and Zucchini

Serves 4

For the stuffed tomatoes:
8 red tomatoes
1 ½ cans (250 g) tuna in oil
2 medium large zucchini
2 garlic cloves
3 Tbsp extra-virgin olive oil
4 Tbsp almonds
parsley
½ red chili pepper
salt and pepper

Preparation time 20 minutes
Cooking time 10 minutes
Difficulty Easy
Calories 318
Wine Bianco D'Alcamo

Wash the tomatoes and slice off the top and bottom so that they stay upright.

1. Empty the tomatoes with a scoop or with a spoon, being careful not to break them (Picture 1). Sprinkle a little salt inside and leave to drain overturned on some paper towels.

2. Wash and trim the zucchini. Cut into small dices and sauté in a non-stick pan with the oil, the whole garlic and the crumbled chili pepper (Picture 2).

3. Cook for 3 minutes and add the tuna crumbled by hand (Picture 3). Season well and add a Tbsp of hot water.

4. Dust with chopped parsley and use to fill the hollow tomatoes (Picture 4). Top with the sliced almonds and bake in a hot oven at 375°F (190°C) for 5 minutes. Serve the hot tomatoes with a crisp surface immediately.

Kitchen tip Add more flavor by blending the zucchini and tuna in a food processor and adding 1 tsp Genoese pesto or 1 tsp black olive tapenade: fill the tomatoes, leave to rest in the refrigerator, and serve cold (in this case, however, the tomato skins must be removed before emptying them).

Warm Salmon
and Potato Salad

Serves 4

For the salad:
1 lb (450 g) fresh salmon
3 yellow potatoes
⅓ lb (150 g) string beans
4 Tbsp extra-virgin olive oil
1 lemon
mixed aromatic herbs (chervil,
   thyme, chives)
pink peppercorns
white peppercorns
salt

Preparation time 25 minutes
Cooking time 20 minutes
Difficulty Easy
Calories 415
Wine Lugana

Place the potatoes with their skins in cold salted water and bring to a boil.

1. Remove the bones from the salmon and finely slice it diagonally, to obtain some wide slices (Picture 1).

2. Blend the lightly salted lemon juice with the oil and the chopped herbs; pour some of the juice over the bottom of a tray lined with plastic wrap and arrange the slices of salmon on top. Cover with more juice (Picture 2) and with the peppercorn. Seal with more plastic wrap and leave to marinate in a refrigerator for 30 minutes.

3. Trim the string beans and boil in salted water for 6 minutes until firm to the bite. Peel the potatoes, still hot, and cut into thick slices (Picture 3).

4. Drain the salmon from the marinade, place on the potatoes and serve with the string beans (Picture 4). The heat of the potatoes will finish cooking the salmon, which has already been marinated in the lemon juice.

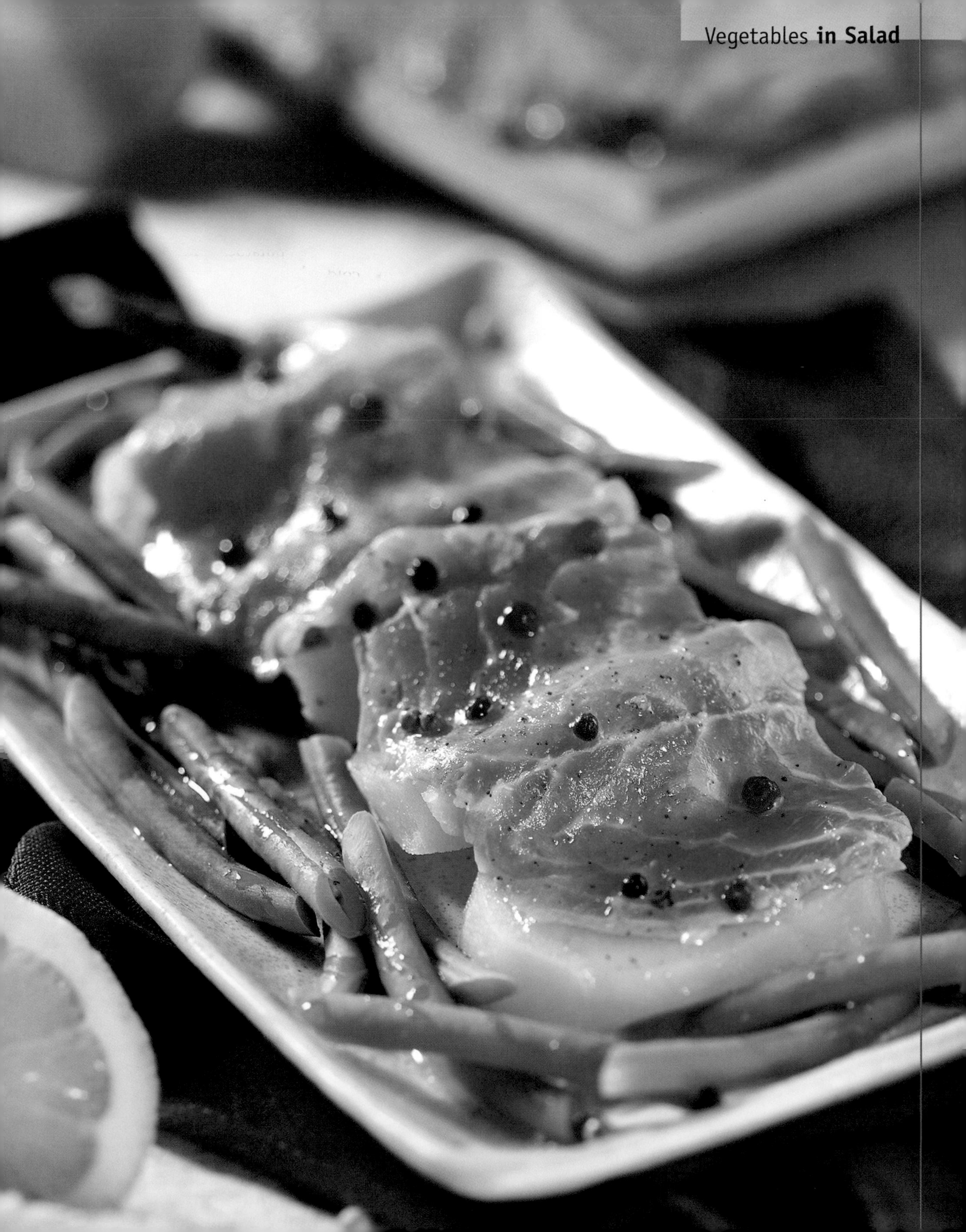

Vegetable **Soups**

Puréed Porcini Mushroom
and Potato Soup

Serves 4

For the soup:

2 medium-small potatoes
⅓ lb (150 g) porcini mushrooms
1 pat butter
2 Tbsp extra-virgin olive oil
1 large shallot
6 ½ cups (1.5 l) vegetable broth
1 thyme sprig
2 slices homemade bread
powdered chili pepper
salt and pepper

Peel the potatoes and cut them into thin slices. Clean the mushrooms with damp kitchen paper and remove the bottom part of the stem.

1. Chop the shallot and simmer in a saucepan with butter and oil. Add a pinch of chili pepper and the potatoes, stirring frequently.

2. Slice the porcini (Picture 1) and add to the potatoes; cook for 3 minutes and cover with the boiling broth (Picture 2). Cook over medium heat for approx. 20 minutes and purée in a blender (Picture 3), dusting with the thyme leaves. Season with salt and pepper.

3. Dice the bread and toast in a hot oven or in a non-stick pan. Serve the porcini soup in individual bowls, with a swirl of raw oil and the crunchy croutons.

Kitchen tip You can sauté the porcini in a separate pan with 1 garlic clove, oil and parsley before adding to the potatoes. Keep some aside for garnishing.

Preparation time 15 minutes
Cooking time 30 minutes
Difficulty Easy
Calories 139
Wine Alto Adige Pinot Nero

1 2 3

Black Eyed Pea
and Artichoke Soup

Serves 4

For the soup:
2 cups (300 g) black-eyed peas
1 celery stalk with leaves
3 artichokes
1 onion
2 garlic cloves
½ cup (150 g) tomato paste
4 Tbsp extra-virgin olive oil
¼ cup white wine
4 slices Tuscan bread
2 rosemary sprigs
1 bay leaf
chili pepper
salt

For the flavored oil:
4 Tbsp extra-virgin olive oil
2 sage leaves

Cook the peas (after leaving them to soak overnight) in plenty of lightly salted water and add 1 bay leaf.

1. Clean the artichokes, remove the tougher outer leaves (Picture 1), the inner choke and dice. Dice the onion and celery and simmer in a saucepan with some oil, the crushed garlic and the artichokes.

2. Drain the peas and add them to the vegetables in the saucepan. Leave to simmer for a few minutes. Add the white wine and the tomato paste and cover with water. Season with salt and cook for about 30 minutes.

3. Warm the extra-virgin olive oil with the shredded sage leaves. Toast the slices of bread under a grill, brush with the sage-flavored oil and place on the bottom of 4 soup plates. Pour the hot soup over the bread, leave to rest for a few minutes and serve dusting with chili pepper to taste.

Interesting to know Black-eyed peas have a distinctive, slightly grassy flavor. They take their name from the small black mark on their skin.

Preparation time 30 minutes
Cooking time 1 hour
Difficulty Easy
Calories 471
Wine Valpolicella

Jerusalem Artichoke
and Shallot Soup

Serves 8

For the soup

1 lb (500 g) jerusalem artichoke
10 whole shallots
⅓ cup (50 g) icing sugar
6 Tbsp extra-virgin olive oil
1 piece lard
2 ½ cups (600 ml) chicken broth
8 small slices of toasted brioche
   bread
2 thyme sprigs
1 Tbsp (10 g) salmon eggs

Preparation time 10 minutes
Cooking time 1 hour and
              30 minutes
Difficulty Medium
Calories 226
Wine Soave

Coat 8 whole shallots with icing sugar, add the thyme sprigs and wrap in a sheet of kitchen foil. Drizzle with a little oil (Picture 1) and close well.

1. Bake in a hot oven at 275°F (140°C) for approx. 1 hour and 20 minutes. Once the shallots are cooked, peel and cut into chunks.

2. Put the piece of lard in a pan with some oil, 2 finely chopped shallots and fry lightly. Clean the artichoke (Picture 2), dice and add to the shallots (Picture 3).

3. Leave to simmer for a few moments and add the hot chicken broth. Season with salt and pepper. Cook for approx. 5 minutes, remove the lard and purée in a blender (Picture 4). Filter the mixture with a strainer.

4. Serve the jerusalem artichoke soup piping hot in a soup plate. Lay the slice of toasted bread in the center and garnish with the pieces of shallot and salmon eggs.

Puréed Fava Bean
and Ham Soup

Serves 4

For the puréed soup:
1 ½ cups (200 g) dried fava beans
1 medium sized yellow potato
4 cups (1 l) light vegetable broth
½ white onion
4 Tbsp extra-virgin olive oil
4 slices (100 g) Parma ham
1 sprig rosemary
salt and pepper

Blanch the fava beans (after leaving them to soak overnight) in salt water for 10 minutes, drain and shell.

1. Chop the onion finely and simmer in a saucepan with the oil (Picture 1). Peel and slice the potato thinly, add to the onion and sauté for 2 minutes.

2. Add the fava beans and season with some salt; cover with the hot broth and leave to cook slowly for 30 minutes, adding the rosemary just before removing from heat. Remove the rosemary and blend with an immersion blender; add some pepper to taste.

3. Cut the prosciutto into thin strips and sauté in a non-stick pan until crispy (Picture 2). Serve the fava bean soup with the prosciutto on the surface.

Kitchen tip To speed up the preparation use shelled dry fava beans that require less soaking time (approx. 6 hours) and that do not need to be blanched before being simmered.

Preparation time 15 minutes
Cooking time 40 minutes
Difficulty Easy
Calories 375
Wine Lagrein Rosato

Puréed Carrot Soup
and Thyme Sautéed Shrimp

Serves 4

For the carrot soup:
1 lb (400 g) carrots
1 medium potato
2 pats butter
½ white onion
16 shrimp
1 Tbsp extra-virgin olive oil
1 garlic clove
thyme
salt and pepper

Peel the onion and chop it up finely; simmer it in saucepan with the butter.

1. Clean the carrots, peel and slice into rounds. Wash the potatoes, peel and slice; add the prepared vegetables to the onion, leave to simmer for 5 minutes and cover with hot water.

2. Cook over medium heat and purée as soon as the vegetables are cooked. Flavor with thyme and salt and pepper to taste.

3. Shell the shrimp, devein (Picture 1) and sauté in a non-stick pan with oil, the clove of garlic, salt and pepper. Place a thin layer of soup on the plates and garnish with the sautéed shrimp.

Kitchen tip Vary the flavor of this dish by replacing the puréed carrots with zucchini, spinach, artichokes or broccoli, according to the season.

Preparation time 20 minutes
Cooking time 25 minutes
Difficulty Easy
Calories 186
Wine Alto Adige Pinot Bianco

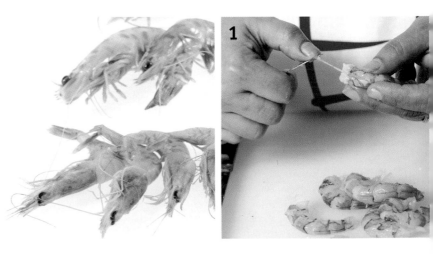

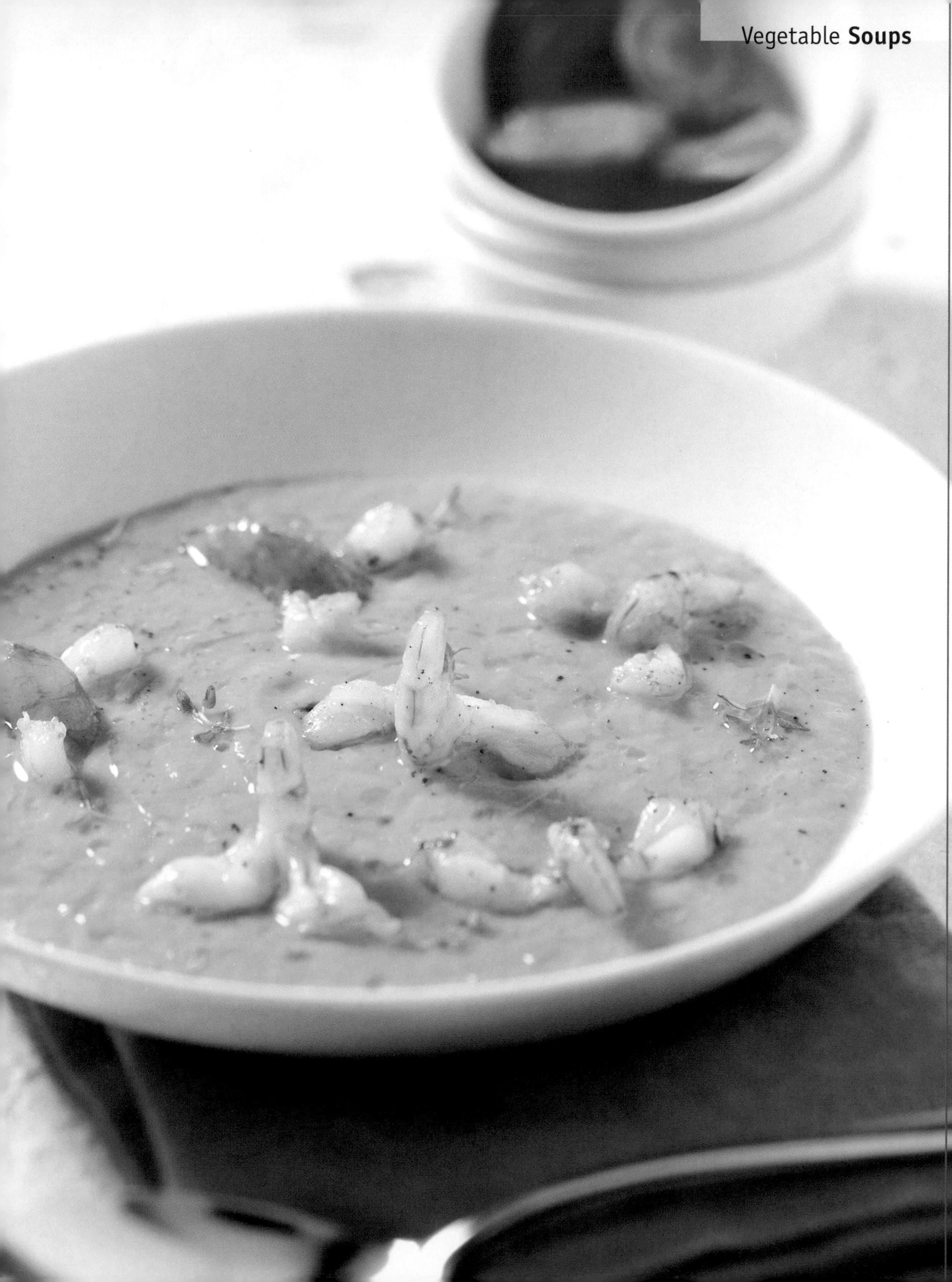

Leek, Potato
and Sautéed Pumpkin Soup

Serves 4

For the pumpkin soup:
½ leek
1 cup (200 g) white rice
1 large potato
⅔ lb (300 g) pumpkin
¼ lb (50 g) mature peppered pecorino
  cheese
vegetable broth
1 garlic clove
3 pats butter
2 Tbsp extra-virgin olive oil
salt and pepper

Julienne the leek (Pictures 1-2-3) and simmer slowly in a saucepan with the butter.

1. Peel the potato, cut into thin slices and add to the leek. Lightly season with salt and pepper and cover with the hot broth. Leave to cook slowly and, as soon as the potatoes are cooked, purée the ingredients together.

2. Remove the rind from the pumpkin, dice it and cook in a saucepan with oil, a clove of garlic and some salt.

3. Cook the rice in the broth and serve in the puréed leeks with the diced pumpkin. Garnish with shavings of pecorino.

Interesting to know Roma rice is one of the 6 traditional types of superfine rice and is especially appreciated in the preparation of a number of regional and traditional dishes. This rice can be replaced by the Arborio variety or by the so-called Comune rice, also known as Originario; this last variety is particularly suitable for preparing soups and desserts.

Preparation time 30 minutes
Cooking time 35 minutes
Difficulty Easy
Calories 410
Wine Trentino Marzemino

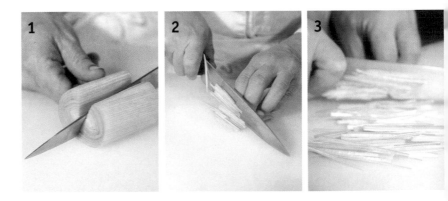

Puréed Pumpkin Soup
with Shrimp and Speck Wraps

Serves 4

For the pumpkin soup:

1 ⅓ lb (600 g) pumpkin flesh
2 shallots
1 pat butter
6 Tbsp extra-virgin olive oil
3 sage leaves
⅓ lb (180 g) potatoes
2 cups (½ l) water
salt and pepper

For the wraps:

⅓ lb (180 g) shrimp
3 thin slices (50 g) speck
2 Tbsp extra-virgin olive oil

Clean the pumpkin and dice the flesh. Peel and dice the potatoes.

1. Peel the shallots, slice thinly and sauté in a saucepan with the oil, butter and sage. Add the pumpkin and the potatoes and season with salt and pepper to taste.

2. Leave to simmer for a few minutes and add the water. Leave to boil over moderate heat for approx. 20 minutes, stirring from time to time.

3. Purée the mixture with an immersion blender to a smooth cream (Picture 1). Leave the purée to bubble for a few more minutes and add a pinch of salt.

4. Shell the shrimp and lay on a working surface. Cut the slices of speck in halves lengthways. Wrap each shrimp in ½ slice speck (Picture 2). Warm the oil in a pan and sauté the shrimp for 2 minutes on each side.

5. Put the pumpkin soup in individual plates. Arrange some sautéed shrimp on the soup. Drizzle with a dash of extra-virgin olive oil and serve immediately.

Preparation time 35 minutes
Cooking time 25 minutes
Difficulty Easy
Calories 340
Wine Collio Tocai Superiore

1   2

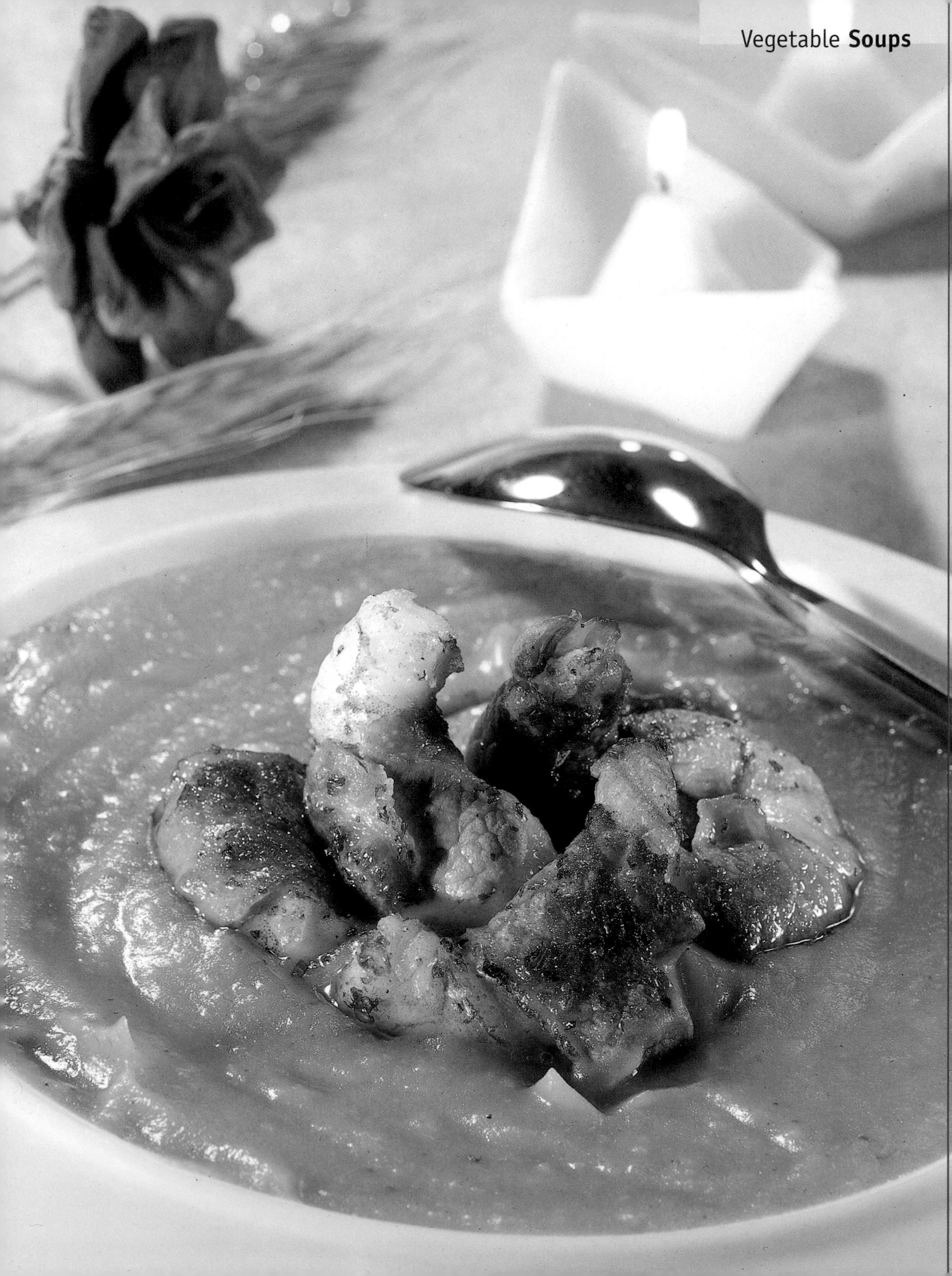

Cold Spicy
Yogurt Soup

Serves 4

For the soup:
2 cups (500 g) plain yogurt
1 green onion
2 stalks white celery
2 Tbsp white vinegar
4 Tbsp extra-virgin olive oil
1 dill sprig
chili pepper
salt

For the toasted bread:
4 slices of white sandwich bread
2 Tbsp mixed herbs

For garnishing
1 sprig wild fennel

R emove the fibrous strings from the celery stalks, clean the onion and slice finely (Picture 1). Cut the other vegetables into pieces and place in a blender with the yogurt, a pinch of chili pepper and ½ teaspoon salt.

1. Purée until smooth and creamy, then add the extra-virgin olive oil, the white vinegar and chopped dill; purée for a few more seconds and put in the refrigerator until serving.

2. Dust the slices of bread with the chopped mixed herbs and press lightly with a rolling pin so that they adhere to the bread.

3. Cut the bread with a round cutter and toast the rounds under an oven grill for a few minutes. Garnish the yogurt soup with some wild fennel leaves.

4. Serve the spicy yogurt soup cold with the toasted herbed bread.

Preparation time 15 minutes
Cooking time 5 minutes
Difficulty Easy
Calories 229
Wine

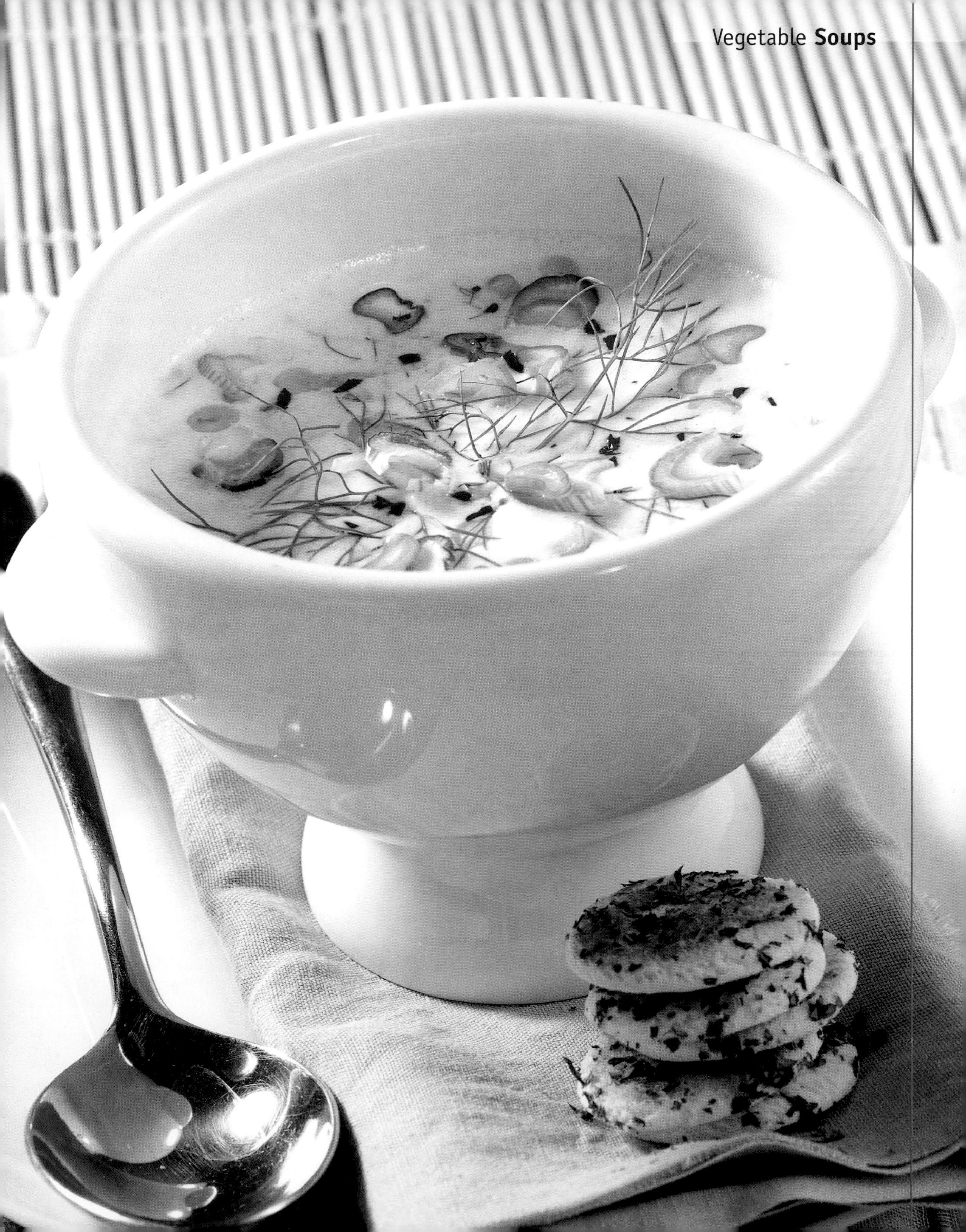

Pinto Bean
and Cauliflower Soup

Serves 4

For the soup:
1 lb (500 g) cauliflower
1 cup (200 g) pinto beans
2 Tbsp extra-virgin olive oil
1 anchovy filet in oil
1 small bunch parsley
1 bay leaf
2 cups (½ l) water
salt

For the flavored oil:
3 Tbsp extra-virgin olive oil
1 dry chili pepper
2 cloves garlic
1 rosemary sprig

Soak the pinto beans overnight, then cook in lightly salted water with the bay leaf for 35-40 minutes.

1. Divide the cauliflower into florets, discarding the toughest part of the stem. Put the anchovy filet with 2 Tbsp of oil in a pan, warm up and add the cauliflower. Season with salt, leave to simmer for a few minutes, then cover with 2 cups (½ l) of water and cook covered over medium heat for 10 minutes.

2. Warm the remaining oil with the sliced cloves of garlic, the crumbled chili and the rosemary in a pan. Leave to rest. When the pinto beans are ready, drain and add to the cauliflower. Leave to simmer for 10-15 minutes.

3. Dust with the chopped parsley and drizzle with the filtered flavored oil. Mix the soup and serve piping hot.

Kitchen tip Serve the soup in terracotta bowls heated in a hot oven, covered with a thin layer of puff pastry that will raise while in the oven.

Preparation time 10 minutes
Cooking time 1 hour and
20 minutes
Difficulty Easy
Calories 240
Wine Merlot

Pumpkin
and Black Cabbage Soup

Serves 4

For the soup:

2 potatoes
¼ pumpkin
7-8 leaves black cabbage
3 Tbsp extra-virgin olive oil
1 garlic clove
1 yellow onion
2 sage leaves
1 rosemary sprig
1 ¼ cups (250 g) cannellini beans
2 cups (½ l) vegetable broth
salt and pepper

Preparation time 20 minutes
Cooking time 35 minutes
Difficulty Easy
Calories 199
Wine Bardolino Chiaretto

Place the garlic, rosemary and sage with some olive oil in a saucepan and leave to simmer.

1. Peel and thinly slice the onion and add to the saucepan after removing the sage and rosemary. Simmer well over low heat.

2. In the meantime, remove the green rind from the pumpkin (Picture 1) and dice the flesh into medium-large chunks. Peel the potatoes and cut into smaller pieces. Add to the saucepan and season with a little salt and pepper. Leave to simmer and add some boiling broth. Leave to cook for 10 minutes.

3. Wash and cut the black cabbage into pieces (Picture 2). Add to the saucepan (Picture 3) and cover with a lid.

4. Purée the beans, previously cooked, add a little broth and pour into the soup (Picture 4). Cook for other 15 minutes and serve.

Kitchen tip Black cabbage is rather rare: it is only available in winter and, even in this season, it isn't always easy to find. For this reason, the black cabbage can be replaced with the more common Savoy cabbage, leaving the flavor almost unaffected.

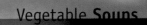

Leek
and Potato Soup

Serves 4

For the soup:
1 cup (200 g) white rice
2 medium potatoes
1 leek
2 slices Colonnata lard
2 Tbsp extra-virgin olive oil
vegetable broth
vegetable oil
salt and pepper

Slice the leek finely, keep some aside and stew the rest in saucepan with the extra-virgin olive oil and a little water for approx. 5 minutes.

1. Finely chop the lard and add to the simmered leek. Peel and slice the potatoes (Picture 1); dice and add to the leek.

2. Simmer for 2 or 3 minutes and add the rice; cover with the hot broth and cook for 18-20 minutes, seasoning with salt and pepper.

3. Warm the oil and fry the leek kept aside. Drain well on paper towels.

4. Serve the leek soup and potatoes piping hot, garnishing the plate with the fried leeks.

Preparation time 15 minutes
Cooking time 30 minutes
Difficulty Easy
Calories 139
Wine Alto Adige Pinot Nero

Savoy Cabbage
and Potato Soup

Serves 4

For the soup:
½ Savoy cabbage
1 large yellow potato
¼ green skinned round pumpkin
1 white onion
1 carrot
1 celery stalk
2 cups (½ l) vegetable broth
4 Tbsp extra-virgin olive oil
1 garlic clove
4 slices unsalted homemade bread
salt and pepper

Cut the onion into thin slices and simmer in a saucepan with the oil and unpeeled garlic.

1. Peel and trim the carrot and remove the seeds and green rind from the pumpkin. Dice the pumpkin and slice the carrot into rounds and add to the garlic and oil.

2. Peel and slice the potato (Picture 1), put it in the saucepan after removing the garlic and sauté for a few minutes, seasoning with salt and pepper. Add some broth or hot water and leave to cook for 20 minutes.

3. In the meantime, wash and julienne the Savoy cabbage and place in saucepan with the other vegetables; cover with a lid and continue to cook for other 20 minutes. Toast the bread and serve with the soup.

Kitchen tip To enhance the flavor of the soup, scatter some mature pecorino cheese over the slices of homemade bread, bake au gratin in oven for a few minutes and place directly on the soup, garnishing with a swirl of extra-virgin olive oil.

Preparation time 25 minutes
Cooking time 40 minutes
Difficulty Easy
Calories 618
Wine Rossese di Dolceacqua

1

Chestnut
and Potato Purée

Serves 4

For the purée:
2 large potatoes
20 chestnuts
2 shallots
3 Tbsp extra-virgin olive oil
1 tsp mustard (slightly hot)
¾ cup (200 ml) vegetable broth
homemade bread
salt and black pepper

Chop the shallots, place in pan and fry with the extra-virgin olive oil over high heat.

1. Add the potatoes, cut into thin slices, and the broth (Picture 1) and cook for 30 minutes on a slow fire.

2. Score the shell off each chestnut with a sharp knife and boil in lightly salted water for 30 minutes. Once cooked, peel, crush and add to the potatoes.

3. Purée the mixture with the mustard and season with salt and pepper. Cut the homemade bread into thin slices and toast under the oven grill. Spread the toasts with the chestnut cream and serve immediately.

Interesting to know Mustard plants belong to the Brassicaceae family: they have a pungent flavor and anti-oxidant properties. There are 2 types of mustard, white and dark. Just like chili peppers, mustard can cause local irritation, therefore those who suffer from stomach or intestine disorders should avoid it.

Preparation time 25 minutes
Cooking time 1 hour
Difficulty Easy
Calories 457
Wine Alto Adige Sylvaner

Chickpea Soup
with Toasted Bread and Sausage

Serves 4

For the soup:

1 cup (200 g) dry chickpeas

2 cloves garlic

1 bay leaf

1 rosemary sprig

1 cup (120 g) chopped celery, carrots
    and onions

¼ cup full-bodied red wine

4 Tbsp extra-virgin olive oil

1 hot chili pepper

8 slices baguette bread

⅓ lb (150 g) luganega sausage

salt

Soak the chickpeas overnight. Cook them in lightly salted water with the bay leaf and 1 garlic clove for approx. 40 minutes.

1. Prepare the chopped vegetables (Pictures 1-2) and sauté in a saucepan with oil and the remaining clove of garlic. Add the chili pepper, the drained chickpeas and leave to simmer for a few minutes. Add the red wine, cover with the vegetable broth and cook for other 20 minutes.

2. Purée ⅓ of the soup and add to the other ingredients. Season to taste and keep warm.

3. Crumble the sausage by hand and sprinkle over the slices of bread; place under a boiler for a few minutes and arrange 2 on each plate.

Interesting to know Chickpeas are linked to an important event in Italian history: the Sicilian Vespers. During a revolt in Palermo in 1282 the word ciceri (chickpeas) became a question of life or death. The French soldiers were not able to say it without pronouncing the final "i" and the Sicilians, who were anxious to slaughter them, forced those suspected of being French to repeat this word: those who couldn't utter the correct sound were sentenced to death.

Preparation time 25 minutes
Cooking time 1 hour
Difficulty Easy
Calories 438
Wine Chianti Classico

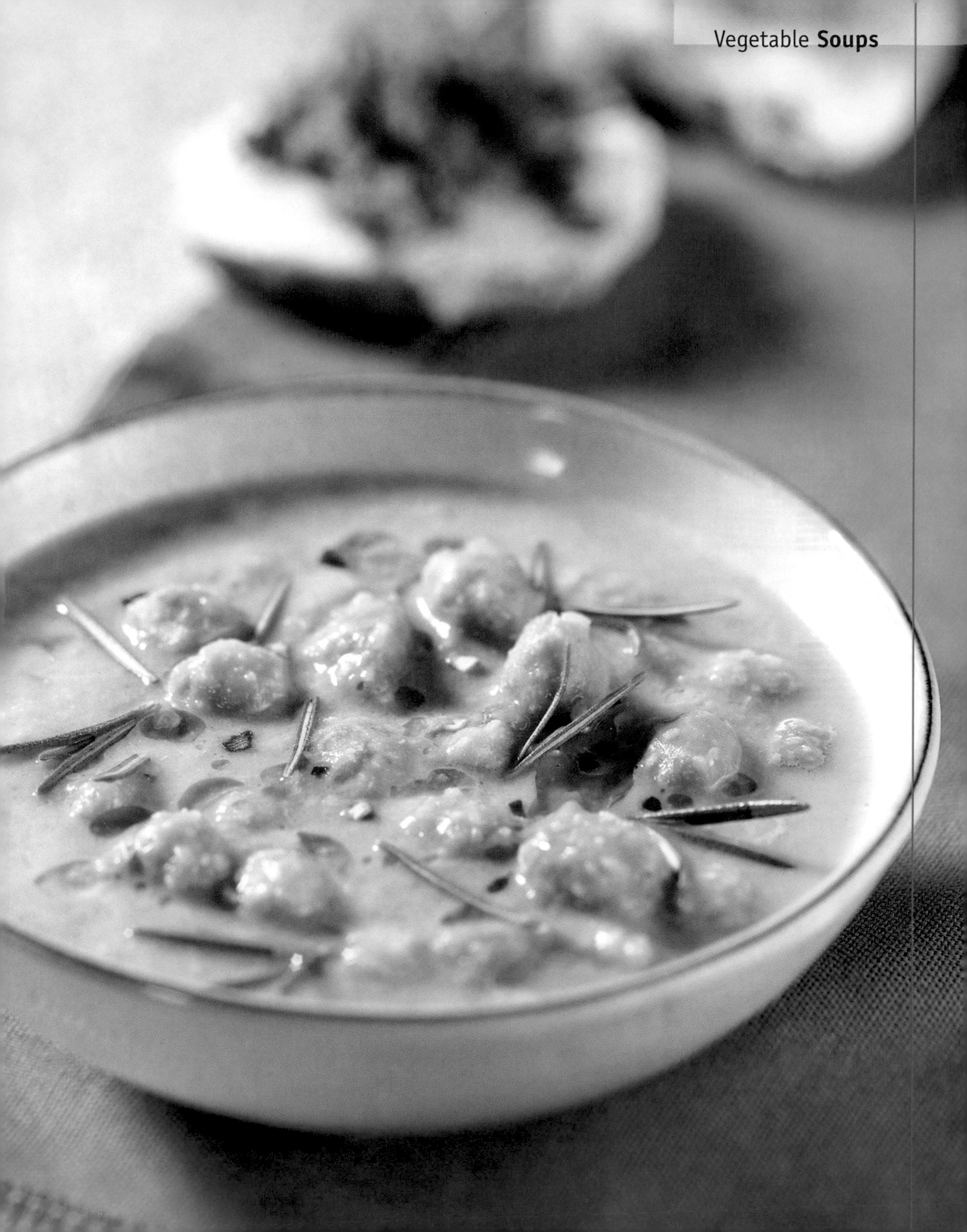

Carrot Soup
with Orange Juice

Serves 6

For the soup:

1 ¼ lb (500 g) carrots

2 oranges

½ onion

2 Tbsp extra-virgin olive oil

1 stalk celery

2 teaspoons parsley

cumin, coriander, ginger and nutmeg

⅓ cup (100 ml) cream

¼ cup white wine

salt

Finely chop the celery, the onion and approx. 1 lb (400 g) of peeled carrots. Sauté all together in a saucepan with 1 Tbsp of extra-virgin olive oil (Picture 1).

1. Add the wine, leave to evaporate and add 4 cups of water and the juice of 2 oranges. Cook for 30 minutes.

2. Purée the mixture, add the cream and leave to reduce for 10 minutes over low heat. Season with the spices and a pinch of salt. Leave to rest for no less than 1 hour.

3. Julienne the remaining carrots and sauté in a pan with some oil for 5 minutes over a high flame.

4. Serve the soup with the crispy carrots and the chopped fresh parsley.

Interesting to know Cumin seeds are commonly used to prepare food. They have a slightly bitter and peppery flavor. Even the sprouts derived from the seeds are used to add flavor to soups. Cumin enhances the appetite, helps digestion and is used to remove bad breath. It also has antiseptic and depurative properties.

Preparation time 25 minutes
Cooking time 50 minutes
Difficulty Easy
Calories 154
Wine Terre di Franciacorta
        Bianco

Spicy Cream of Amaranth Soup
with Celery Root and Pine Nuts

Serves 4

For the cream of amaranth:
1 ⅓ cups (250 g) amaranth grain
½ lb (200 g) celery root
⅓ cup (100 ml) fresh cream
2 Tbsp (20 g) pine nuts
5-6 cardamom seeds
2 cloves
3 Tbsp extra-virgin olive oil
celery leaves
salt and pepper

Peel and dice the celery root. Open the cardamom seeds and crush the dark seeds inside, together with the cloves, reducing to powder.

1. Rinse the amaranth in a fine sieve and place in a saucepan with the celery root and the crushed spices. Season with salt, cover with 2 ⅓ cup (600 ml) of water and cook covered for 30 minutes.

2. Toast the pine nuts in an oven or in a pan and keep aside. Once the cream is cooked, add the fresh cream (Picture 1), season with salt and pepper to taste and pour into soup plates. Garnish with the pine nuts, celery leaves and a drizzle of olive oil.

Interesting to know Amaranth belongs to the Amaranthaceous family, and can be eaten in grains or puffed. It has a pleasant flavor and can be added to vegetables and mixed with other cereals, like rice, barley, millet and spelt, or used as an excellent base in the preparation of baby food. Rich in high quality and easily assimilated proteins, it contains high amounts of lysine (an essential amino acid that other cereals usually do not have), calcium, phosphorus, magnesium and iron. Amaranth is gluten-free and, therefore, can be eaten by those who have food allergies.

Preparation time 15 minutes
Cooking time 35 minutes
Difficulty Easy
Calories 312
Wine Friuli Verduzzo

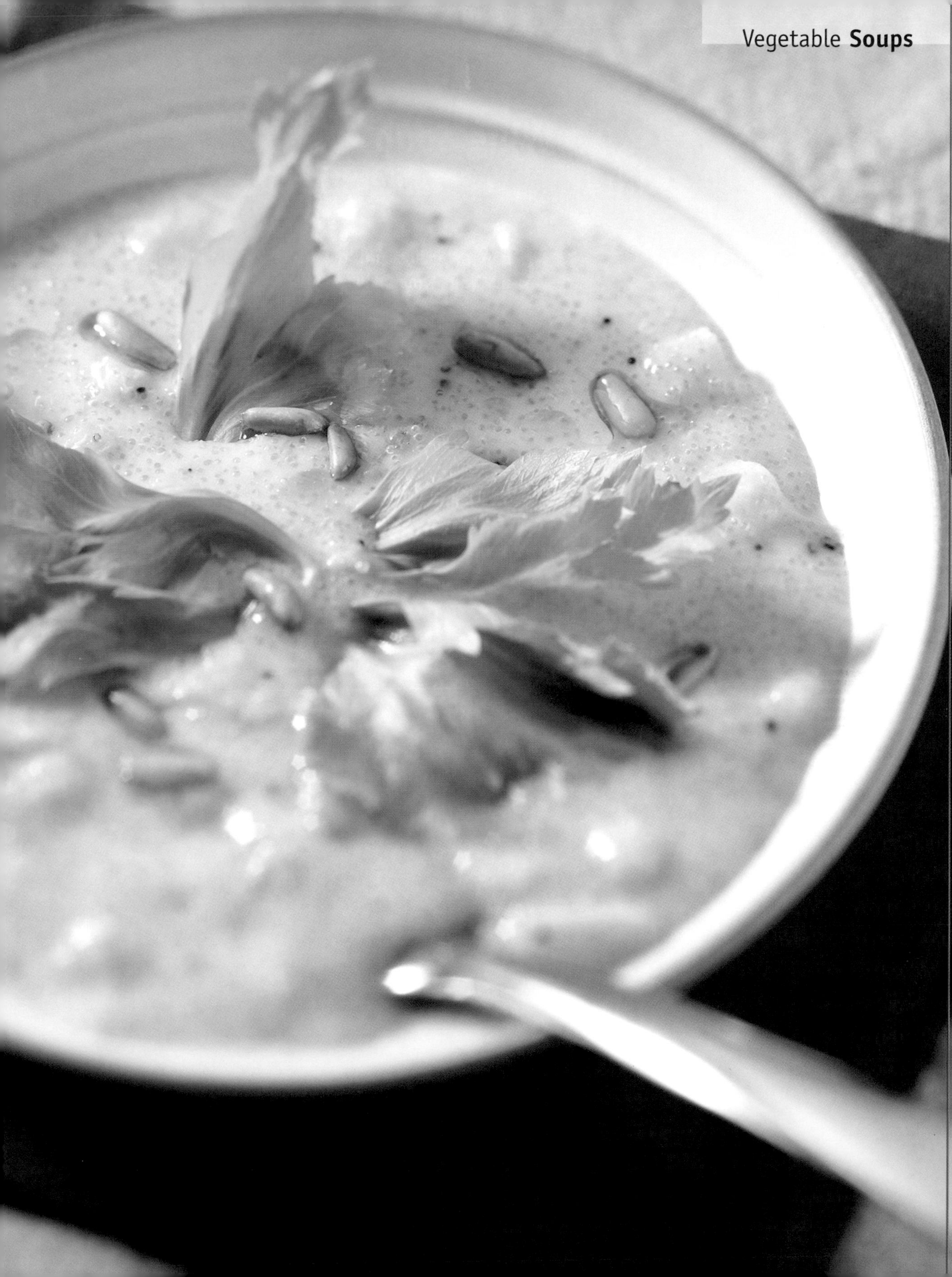

Wine Soup
with Fried Vegetable Strudel

Serves 4

For the soup:
1 pat butter
1 egg yolk
2 Tbsp cream
2 shallots
½ cup white wine
2 cups (½ l) meat or vegetable broth
salt and pepper

For the strudel:
1 ¼ cups (150 g) all-purpose flour
1 egg
extra-virgin olive oil
vegetable oil for frying
salt

For the filling:
⅕ lb (50 g) mushrooms
1 potato
1 carrot
1 stalk celery
1 garlic clove
extra-virgin olive oil
parsley
basil
salt

Preparation time 40 minutes
Cooking time 25 minutes
Difficulty Medium
Calories 294
Wine Roero Arneis

Chop the shallots and stew in a saucepan with the butter; add the white wine, reduce and add the broth.

1. Mix the cream with the egg yolk, add to the soup and purée well. Season with salt and pepper.

2. Prepare the strudel by mixing the flour, egg, salt and extra-virgin olive oil. Add some water until the dough gains the right texture. Work well until the dough becomes smooth and consistent, then roll it out into a thin sheet (Picture 1).

3. Wash and clean the vegetables and julienne them, sauté in pan with the oil and garlic (Picture 2), and finish with the chopped parsley, basil and salt.

4. Spread the vegetables on some pastry rectangles (Picture 3) and roll them up to form the strudels. Fry in plenty of vegetable oil and drain on kitchen paper.

5. Serve the soup, placing the strudel cut in half in the center.

184

Puréed Onion
and Potato Soup

Serves 4

For the soup:
⅔ stick (75 g) butter
4 white onions
2 potatoes
1 Tbsp all-purpose flour
4 eggs
6 cups (1 ½ l) milk
2 cups (½ l) water
parmesan cheese
pecorino cheese
salt and pepper

For the croutons:
1 Tbsp extra-virgin olive oil
½ baguette

Peel and dice the onions. Brown the onions in a pan with the butter, add salt and pepper and dust with flour. Stir constantly to prevent the flour from darkening.

1. Add the potatoes cut into pieces (Picture 1), then pour in the milk and water. Leave to cook for approx. half an hour, stirring from time to time (Picture 2).

2. Prepare the croutons while the soup is cooking: dice the baguette, place in a tray and drizzle with a little oil. Bake the pieces of bread au gratin for a few minutes until golden.

3. Purée the soup with an immersion blender until smooth and creamy. Grate the pecorino cheese and the parmesan and add to the soup.

4. Place 1 egg on the bottom of each soup plate or terracotta bowl and smother with the onion and potato soup (Picture 3). Serve piping hot with the croutons.

Preparation time 15 minutes
Cooking time 30 minutes
Difficulty Easy
Calories 617
Wine Pinot Grigio del Piave

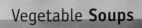